Ruth Tayl...

Christmas from Joanne
76

THE
LAST
EAGLE
THE STORY OF KHAN

Books by Ben East
SURVIVAL
DANGER!
THE SILENCE OF THE NORTH
    (WITH OLIVE FREDRICKSON)
THE LAST EAGLE

THE LAST EAGLE

THE STORY OF KHAN

BY BEN EAST

CROWN PUBLISHERS, INC.

NEW YORK

Library of Congress Catalog Card Number: 73-91511

Manufactured in the United States of America
Published simultaneously in Canada by General Publishing Company Limited
Designed by Ruth Smerechniak

By design, the eagles in this story bear the closest possible likeness to their living counterparts; but the human characters are entirely fictitious, and any resemblance they may seem to have to actual persons, living or dead, is unintentional.

ACKNOWLEDGMENTS

I owe thanks to a number of people for the information I have drawn on, notably the late Arthur Cleveland Bent, dean of American bird writers, whose *Life Histories of North American Birds of Prey,* published by the Smithsonian Institution in 1937, contains a rich lode of fascinating factual material and many wonderful anecdotes. My special thanks go, too, to Sergej Postapulsky of the University of Wisconsin, who for many years has carried on extensive studies of the eagle population of the Great Lakes; and to James Grier, formerly of the Laboratory of Ornithology at Cornell University and now living at Waterloo, Iowa, who in 1972 accomplished the unheard-of feat of hatching three young golden eagles by artificial insemination.

His adult birds were all ten to twelve years old and accustomed to captivity. He prevailed on the two males to ejaculate semen into the palm of his hand and persuaded or forced the females to open their cloacal orifices in readiness to receive the semen. The males copulated on his arm a total of 468 times between December and April. One female postured voluntarily for breeding. It proved necessary to inject the semen into the other forcibly with a syringe.

Obviously both male and female birds considered Grier a mate. He even worked with them in nest building and in incubating the eggs.

The two females laid nine eggs, from which three eaglets hatched.

Grier says jokingly that although he has not been charged with polygamy he is probably the only individual, bird or human, to have mated successfully with four eagles in a single season.

I should like to make one other acknowledgment, to the memory of my friend Walter Hastings, who was the first staff photographer of the Michigan Department of Conservation and one of the finest amateur ornithologists I have known.

It was with him that I banded my first three eagles; that I spied on nesting loons and photographed the hard-to-find newly hatched chicks of ruffed grouse; and with him that I visited the crowded gull and tern colonies on the unpeopled islands of the Great Lakes, among the most interesting bird cities I have found anywhere, not even excepting the teeming sea-cliff colonies of murres and kittiwakes, auklets and puffins along the coast of Alaska.

On one of those Great Lakes islands, Little Shoe, a long, curving reef of gravel at the north end of Lake Michigan, I have seen the eggs of the beautiful Caspian tern, laid on the bare shingle, so close together that a man could have walked the whole length of the reef, from one end to the other, and crushed eggs underfoot at every step. Once on that island Hastings and I found eggs by the hundreds washed up in windrows when the seas of a storm swept in across the low beach.

These and many other birding adventures I shared with him. He was a good companion and a camera hunter extraordinary, and my memories of him are wonderful indeed.

For all the eagles I have known
and for the splendid wilderness
whose incarnate symbol they were

CONTENTS

PREFACE

This story is fiction, and I have taken the liberties to which a writer of fiction is entitled.

I have toyed with place names and rearranged locations to suit my fancy. There are no Sleeping Bear Mountains on the south shore of Lake Superior, and no Siskowet Lake. The Laughing Whitefish is not as big a river as I have made it here, nor does it flow into Superior where I have placed it.

But there is a Laughing Whitefish and there are mountains, the Porcupines, as wild and roadless as I have talked about. There is even a lake overlooked by a sheer cliff, and a river running from it down a beautiful valley.

As for the site of the Great Nest, there is such a ledge and an ancient pine that looks down from a dizzying height. Years ago I knew another nest like this one, in another pine that crashed finally in a spring gale.

There was another Great Nest, too, real and not imagined, but it was built in a tall hickory beside Lake Erie, seven hundred miles to the south, and it overlooked cornfields and pastureland rather than wilderness.

I think the reader will be likely to raise one central question. If the story is invented, and it is, how faithful is it to known fact?

The ways of the eagles that people these pages are genuinely the ways of their kind. To the best of my knowledge, there is no episode here that is untrue to eagle behavior. I have written fiction but I have not knowingly misrepresented facts.

One final word. The ominous prediction that I have implied

in the title of this book and detailed at the end of the story is mine alone. I cannot claim to know whether it will come true. That it will not is devoutly to be hoped, but there is sound reason to fear that it may.

Holly, Michigan
December, 1973

THE
LAST
EAGLE

THE GREAT NEST

The white-headed she eagle left her nest as morning light began to stain the eastern sky with gray and saffron.

Her departure was swift and silent. She spread her great wings—they spanned almost eight feet from tip to tip—leaped off the rim of the platform, dipped down in an arc from the green top of the aerie pine, planed upward to gain altitude, and turned toward the river.

Her mate, perched in a lookout tree a hundred yards from the nest, watched her go. He called to her—a series of low chittering notes—then tipped from his tree and followed the shore of the lake in the opposite direction.

For both of them this was a hunting flight, the first of the morning. They would patrol the lake edge and follow the turnings of the river until they found and killed food, not for themselves but for the three downy gray fledglings back at the aerie.

Not until the eaglets, hungry and clamorous from the foodless night, had breakfasted would the old birds hunt for their own need.

The she eagle was first to take prey. Flying effortlessly a few hundred feet above the treetops, turning as the river wound, seeing everything beneath her in the brightening light of morning, not with eyes like those of a human but with marvelously keen sight that brought earth and water close as if she looked through powerful binoculars, she scanned the river and its margin with minute diligence. She listened as she watched, but her eyes rather than her sense of hearing would lead her to the kill she sought.

Behind her, in the shallow bay where the Laughing Whitefish River flowed from the lake, a loon called, its wild rolling laughter echoing hauntingly back from the timbered ridges. The eagle heard, tilted vertically in the air, came about and made a short, tight circle back toward the sound of the loon's cry. Then she thought better of it, perhaps because she knew that her mate was hunting in that direction. She came back on course and followed the river again.

The Laughing Whitefish left Siskowet Lake as a mountain stream, slicing down rock chutes, brawling around water-worn blocks of ancient lava, plunging through rapids. A few miles below the lake it broke out of the mountains in a high and lacy waterfall. Just beyond, dammed by the low dike of an ancient beach line, it widened into a shallow lake. The rest of the way to Lake Superior it flowed in wide curves across the coastal plain, deep and dark. Where it lost itself in the big lake, cedars leaned from the bank, giants that had been young trees when the first Jesuit missionaries came that way in birchbark canoes, with Indian paddlers.

The she eagle flew above the falls at treetop height, and in the shallow lake beyond she sighted the fish. It was a medium-sized northern pike, lying just under the surface, among ropelike strands of pondweed that floated up from the bottom. The pike

itself was waiting for food—small perch or suckers that might come drifting among the green ropes of the weed. It lay motionless, its long torpedo-shaped body, pointed head, and tooth-studded jaws giving it a curiously ominous and evil look. It took no note of the eagle, coming swiftly in the air.

She saw it and slanted instantly into a steep dive toward the water. Her great wings flailed the air twice to gain speed, then she folded them back against her body and stooped like a dark meteor, falling almost vertically. At the last instant she tilted and braked and her powerful yellow talons dropped like landing gear.

She struck the water with a splash that sent feet and legs down where the pike lay basking, and her claws locked into the back of the fish like curved steel clamps. She rose with heavy flapping and turned back toward the aerie, carrying the dying pike with one foot.

Miles away, along the lake, the male eagle also sighted prey. Below him, in the shore thickets, a hermit thrush had struck notes as pure as a silver bell into the silence of the spring morning, and farther off, in evergreen timber, a crow-sized pileated woodpecker had called stridently. But he had flown on, giving no heed to either.

He saw no fish. What caught his eyes finally was a small brown animal, long and slender and sinuous as a snake, that darted along the water's edge trailed by four smaller things of its own kind.

The movements of the she mink were swift and nervous, and while the eagle watched her she was not still for a fraction of a second. She darted from one rock to another, vanished beneath the trunk of a tree that had fallen and drowned its top in the water, came into sight again, leaped to the upturned roots of the tree, left them and flashed across the narrow beach. Behind her the four young ran and darted, restless and fast as the mother.

When the eagle stooped on her and she saw it coming there was no time to seek safety for the family and herself in some

shoreline cranny, even had she chosen flight instead of battle—
and that would not have been likely, for she came of a clan of
savage and courageous animals, the weasels. In their veins for a
thousand generations had run blood that did not know the meaning of fear. No matter what the odds, threatened, she was far
more likely to stand and fight than to flee.

She dodged behind a rock as the eagle reached for her, and
the four young had time to scramble out of sight under the fallen
tree.

The eagle landed on the ground, no more than its own
wingspread from her, and she did not wait for it to attack. Instead she leaped at it, snarling and screaming in insane rage. And
now the small arena where they fought was foul with the smell
of weasel musk, a stench as offensive to humans as any animal
smell on earth.

It had no effect on the eagle, however. He would kill the
mink and feed on her if he could, as he had many times killed
her next of kin, the equally bad-smelling skunk.

He struck at the screeching animal with his heavy beak, but
it dodged and leaped away. He lifted clear of the ground in a
swift effortless leap that was helped by his wings, and reached
with his talons, but again the mink was too fast. It moved with
the supple grace of flowing water, its long neck and snakelike
head flashing toward the big and dangerous bird that outweighed
it four to one.

Slowly the eagle drove it back across the beach to the shelter
of a big rock, and from there, when the bird came close enough,
the mink launched itself with a final shrill scream. It struck at
the bird's throat and sank its teeth deep, trying for the big life-
vein in the immemorial fashion of all the weasels.

Only the heavy plumage of the eagle saved his life in that
instant.

He tore at the mink and she released her hold and slashed
again. This time her teeth locked deep in the muscles of his
breast, and then the bird's talons closed in her back, thrusting
through the spine and far into the lungs and piercing the heart.

The mink writhed and died, still fast to its foe. The death grip held while the eagle ripped open the underbelly and tore away flesh and skin until only the head and a flap of tattered fur were left. For more than a year that bleaching skull would hang there, half hidden in the eagle's breast plumage, held fast by its teeth, a souvenir of the battle and a ghoulish amulet. Not that man would ever see and record it, for in that year and for many years to come no man would ever be that close to the eagle.

Partly because of hunger and battle rage, and partly because this was not prey that he wanted to carry back to the eaglets in the aerie, he fed on the spot, tearing pieces of red flesh away from the fur and bones and gulping them down. From their hiding place beneath the log the young mink watched, unaware that they were beginning the ordeal of slow death from hunger, a dying that would take many days to finish.

Back at the aerie, when the she eagle tilted away to her hunting and her mate followed, three eaglets awakened from their night of sleepy torpor, stretched, and relieved themselves of excreta.

From the time they had been able to raise their bodies on weak and uncertain legs, when they were only a day or two old, they had followed a ritual of eliminating, a ritual bedded deep in their ancestral bloodline and one that kept the nest sanitary and safeguarded its occupants against disease.

When the need came to void they stumbled backward to the edge of the dry grass that lined the shallow cup of the nest, elevated their almost naked rumps as high as they could and expelled their ordure forcibly in a liquid stream. Because they were fed little save fish, it was the consistency and color of thin whitewash. The sticks and twigs that formed the rim of the big platform, and a circle of ground below, were whitened with this liquid lime, but the pad of soft grass where the eaglets slept and fed was almost spotlessly clean.

The three had hatched toward the end of April. It was now

early May. They were still soft and helpless chicks, barely able to stand, half naked, clothed only in thin gray down on their bodies and a coat of white down, slightly thicker, on their heads. One was three days older than the next born, who was four days older than the third, and there was a corresponding difference in size among them. The oldest was a male, the others, females.

In March, when the two old birds had completed their annual task of repairing and adding to the nest in the tall pine, the she eagle had laid her first egg on the soft lining in the saucerlike hollow.

The day was raw and cold, with a north wind blowing down the lead-colored sky, and before noon wet snow began to fall, lightly at first, then in a thick white smother that hid the land like a curtain.

But the egg was safe. The she eagle had not left it after it was laid. It lay now in the dry center of the nest, warm and safe under the plumage of her breast. Long before the snow stopped at nightfall she was blanketed with it, hardly more than a white lump on the platform, but still the egg rested safely beneath her. At daybreak the male eagle came to the nest, squealed softly to her, and when she lifted into flight to hunt for the day's first meal he sidled into place behind her, so that the egg was not exposed to the cold spring wind for as long as a minute. Thereafter the two birds would take turns at the long, patient task of incubating, a task that would take thirty-five days.

True to the ways of the raptor clan to which she belonged, the she eagle had waited three days before laying the second egg and four more before she completed her clutch of three. With few exceptions, that is the practice of all eagles, hawks, and owls. And all of them cover the eggs once the first one is laid, and brood while they continue to produce others.

That delay accounted for the differences in size of the three eaglets. It also lessened the chances that the youngest bird would survive and grow to adulthood, for the bigger fledglings naturally

were stronger and more clamorous, claimed more than their share of food, and might attack the smallest with the savagery of all birds of prey if she provoked their anger.

When the three young birds awakened that May morning, the remains of the previous day's hunting by their parents still lay beside them near the rim of the nest. There was a big sucker, as yet untouched, and a small sunfish with head and entrails eaten.

Whatever was brought to the aerie, fish or duck or squirrel, was torn apart and given to them in bits, bill to bill. Weeks would pass before they were strong enough to rend their own food.

The nest on which this feeding and the other activities of spring, including the mating of the parents, was taking place was in itself a marvelous and almost incredible thing.

It had had its beginning thirty years before, when a newly mated pair of five-year-old eagles had come to the big pine and chosen it for their site.

The Sleeping Bear Mountains rose from the south shore of Lake Superior in an abrupt disarray of timbered peaks and ridges, without order but mist-veiled and very beautiful. The slope fronting on the big lake had been logged years before, and young birch and aspen had regrown there, but because of the inaccessibility of the mountains beyond the first ridge the rest had escaped the ax, so that now there lay a broad belt of rugged wilderness twenty miles long and half as wide, roadless and pristine. There were trees in the valleys that three men could barely reach around.

Siskowet Lake lay in a narrow slot in these mountains three miles inland from the Superior beach, across high ridges that rose like giant terraces. The last of these barrier ridges fell to the shore of the lake in a vertical escarpment five hundred feet high, making Siskowet difficult of access save by way of the river that ran out its lower end.

At the top of the escarpment, eons before, a great slab of

rock had broken away, leaving a narrow ledge that angled down, wide enough for a footpath. Twenty feet below the rim it ended in a saucerlike shelf as big as an average house. Moss made a soft green carpet there, and along the lip of the shelf kinnikinnick spread and bore its lovely red berries.

Almost two hundred years before, a pine seed had drifted on the wind and come to rest in the moss. When the spring rains came it sprouted and sent its rootlet hairs down into the shallow soil. Probing in the dark, they found tiny crevices and anchored themselves, and the miracle that is the growth of all living things began. The pine rested now on a skein of roots each thicker than a human thigh, wedged firmly in deep cracks, and its green crown stood more than a hundred feet above the ground. It leaned in toward the cliff at a slight angle, but from its outer branches, had a visitor ventured there, he could have looked down through half a thousand feet of empty space into the clear water of the lake.

The trunk rose straight and clean, after the fashion of white pines, but it was old and hollow now, so that an ax blow struck against it would have rung like a dull drum. No one knew that, however, for no ax had ever been laid upon it.

The trunk went up eighty feet without a branch. There it divided into a massive three-pronged fork. One spring, long ago, a foraging squirrel had gnawed away the tender bud at the tip of the terminal twig, leaving three lateral twigs to turn up and become triple trunks. There the first branches began, and it was in that fork, three decades earlier, that the young eagles had begun their nest.

They worked at it together, gathering dead sticks and branches and placing them carefully and firmly to make the beginnings of a structure that would endure longer than either of them would live.

Many of the branches they picked up from the ground, like fagots. Now and then, overcome with the sheer joy of flight, they chose a dead branch still fixed to its tree, plunging on it as they would plunge on prey, striking it in full dive with the mailed fists of their feet to break it off, and then carrying it to the nest site in uninterrupted flight.

Some of the sticks they collected were only twigs. Some were dry branches almost as long as the spread of their own wings. All this material they laid and twined and wove, using feet and bill, to form a stout parapet four or five feet across. The circle within the parapet they filled with smaller sticks and with the dry stalks of goldenrod and fireweed.

At least once or twice each day they gave over their work to circle high above the ridges in a graceful nuptial dance, turning and screaming at each other in wild ardor. At the end they came down to the nest, or to a bare tree branch nearby, and mated.

When the platform of the nest was three feet high it satisfied them. They added a lining of finer and softer material made up of dry grass and the Usnea moss that hung in streamers from nearby spruce trees. They hollowed the lining at the center, and there the hen laid her first clutch of two round white eggs, at an interval of two days, and began to brood them.

That was the beginning of the massive structure that would, years later, come to be known as the Great Nest.

Eagles, but not the same pair continuously, had used it all the springs since. The two that built it had nested there for a dozen successive years. Each spring in March they came back from the softer land to the south where they had wintered, and went to work at repairing and enlarging their aerie. They built it up as they had built it originally, until it bulked in the fork of the pine as tall as a man and almost as wide, a compact, sturdy thing with a weight of more than a ton.

Then there came a time when the male of the pair returned alone at the end of winter. In a small bay of a sprawling man-made impoundment, a thousand miles away, in December, a duck hunter had watched the female eagle soar lazily toward the decoys that bobbed in front of his blind.

For all her keen vision, when she came close she mistook

the wooden blocks for live birds, slanted down and gripped one in her talons. Before she could rise clear of the water the hunter killed her with a single charge of shot.

So the male made his wandering spring flight north alone. He reached the aerie and began the annual task of building. But he worked only halfheartedly.

Then, as the spring migration of waterfowl and other birds flowed north around him, one cold March morning he spied a distant creature of his own kind in the sky and flew to meet it, ready to drive off an intruder or court a new mate, as the case might be.

The lone migrant was a young female, left mateless, like himself, in the winter. He wooed her down with graceful wing dances and screams of wild longing, led her to his aerie, and when she crouched to signify she was ready they coupled and went on with the work that needed to be done.

That she eagle was the grandmother of the three fledglings now growing in the Great Nest. The male vanished on the winter flight a few years after they had mated, and following the ways of her kind she mated with a younger male before she started north, leading him with her back to the home aerie.

Then she was killed in turn, and the male remated, and life at the nest went on. By that process of succession three different she eagles had brooded here.

At the end of each winter, when a pair returned to the pine ·on the cliff, they repaired the nest and built it higher, so that it now filled the fork to almost twice the height of a tall man, and the same man could have lain in comfort outstretched across its top. Its weight was not less than three or four tons. In all the places where eagles nested, they had not built a sky castle more splendid.

KHAN

Well fed, and sheltered from the spring rains by the widespread wings of the female, the young eagles grew fast. And as they grew the difference in size between the two older ones became less conspicuous. But the youngest of the brood, a female, remained smaller and weaker than the other two.

The parent eagles, like all their kind, lacked the instinct possessed by almost all smaller birds to divide equitably among the fledglings the food they brought to the nest. The two older eaglets, because they were stronger and more clamorous, demanded and got the lion's share of every meal, fish or duck or whatever it might be, at first demanding it from the bills of the parents and then, when they were able to rend their own food, standing over it, hissing, warning off all trespass, gobbling bites of flesh until they were sated.

The smallest eaglet, bullied and half starved, had a stunted look, and her movements about the platform were far less strong and sure than those of the other two.

The gray down of the natal days of all three had given way to dark brown plumage that covered them save for their strong curved bills and yellow feet and the lower shanks of the legs. There was as yet no hint of the snow-white heads and tails they would acquire as adult eagles, in their fourth or fifth summer.

But the male was curiously marked with white in places where none belonged. He carried a broad, irregular patch of it, shaped like a blunt arrowhead, in the center of his breast, narrower bands near the leading edge of each wing, and splashes of white on his upper thighs.

Four generations back there had been in his ancestry a one-in-half-a-million rarity—an albino female, milk white from bill to toes.

Like all birds and animals carrying the strange recessive genes of albinism, she was under severe handicaps from the time she left the natal nest. Other eagles were disposed to reject her as not one of them. Falcons and ospreys singled her out for attack. Worst of all, her eyes, bright pink under the beetling brows where the blood showed through the unpigmented irises, were not capable of the keen and perfect vision of a normal eagle, so that her hunting, her every search for food, suffered.

But she lived to mate with a normal male in her fourth summer, and brooded and reared nestlings twice before she stooped to her death at a fish too heavy to lift, a sturgeon four times her own weight. She locked her talons in its spine and could not free them, and at the end of a brief struggle she was dragged beneath the water and drowned.

It was that taint of albinism, coming down from her diluted by the blood of many dark eagles, that gave this strong fledgling the strange, out-of-place white feathers in his wings and legs and breast.

The eaglets were close to two months old, with bodies

nearly the size of a farmyard rooster's, when Dave Barrows saw them for the first time.

Barrows was thirty years old that spring, young and eager, with the long years of college behind him, a young and pretty wife whom he adored, and an ambition that had goaded and directed his life since boyhood. It was also an ambition that he was now on the way to achieving. He had just become head of a newly created department of ornithology at the University of Lake Superior, two hundred miles to the east of the Sleeping Bears.

Birds and the study of their ways had fascinated him as far back as he could remember. Through his country boyhood he had ferreted out many of their secrets. He had found brooding hen woodcocks on their nests, so perfectly camouflaged by their marvelous plumage that, gathering trailing arbutus, he had put his hand on them and felt their soft warmth under his touch before he knew they were there.

He had seen a male bittern, the thunderpump bird of his farm neighbors, in the rare strutting display of the lacy and beautiful white plumes that adorned its shoulders in breeding season. That was something many professional birdmen had never witnessed.

He had watched mother killdeer undertake to decoy intruders away from their nests by a broken-wing act, rolling over and over on the ground, dragging a wing and uttering low cries of fright and pain, only to fly off once they had been followed far enough.

He had even found the miraculous nest of a hummingbird, jeweled sprite of the bird world. It was a tiny cup saddled on a low branch, a nest so small that a silver quarter laid on its rim would not drop into the deep bowl, and it had been disguised with flecks of lichen bound in place with spider web, bearing marvelous resemblance to a mossy knot.

The year he entered college he and a friend had acquired a peregrine falcon, a young eyas bird taken from the nest. They had trained and flown her, reveling in her grace in the air, her unbelievable speed in flight, her hunting skill, the precision of her deadly stooping, and above all, the proud wild ways she never lost despite her readiness to come to the wrist.

It was in part because of his five-year association with that splendid hawk that Barrows felt a particular interest in and admiration for the raptors, the fierce winged hunters. Now that he had at last a secure place in the life work he meant to follow, he would make them his specialty, the foremost object of his observation and study.

On one score his mind was made up. He would be no desk ornithologist, poring over the dry study skins of birds, studying likenesses and differences, deciding the fine shadings of avian classification. That would be part of his job, of course, but so far as he could he meant to be a field scientist, studying the behavior of living birds.

For a beginning, he set himself the task of acquiring as much knowledge as he could about the eagles of the region. It was in that frame of mind that he saw for the first time the bulky nest in the tall pine overlooking Siskowet Lake.

Human intruders were a rarity in the life of this eagle family. The climb to the top of the ridge that terminated in the cliff was steep and hard, on deer trails that wound through thimbleberry thickets or over tangles of blowdown timber. Few persons were aware of the existence of the nest.

Deer hunters saw it occasionally in autumn, when the eagles were absent, and wondered at its great bulk and look of solidness. Now and then a trout fisherman made his way up the Laughing Whitefish above the falls and reached Siskowet, and if the massive platform in the pine at the top of the escarpment caught his eye, he too wondered.

Apart from these infrequent visitations, the eagle family had had almost no contact with man, which suited them perfectly.

It was Reino Tormala, a Finnish friend of Barrows given to trout fishing every hour of his spare time, who told him about the aerie. Tormala had gone by boat to the mouth of the Laughing Whitefish in May of that year, when the spawning run of steelhead trout was swarming into the river from Lake Superior. From other fishermen he met there, men who lived on the southern edge of the Sleeping Bears, Tormala had heard about the huge eagle nest on the cliff above Siskowet Lake.

He reported it to Dave as soon as he got home. "From what they told me, it's a big one, in a class by itself," he said.

"Let's hike in there and have a look," Barrows proposed.

When they climbed to the top of the last steep terrace below the rim of the escarpment and the aerie came in sight, Barrows pulled up short.

By that time he had visited half a dozen eagle nests, climbing to them to photograph and band the fledgling young, but he had seen no nest remotely like this one for height and bulk. He thought of it in that first minute as the Great Nest, and that was how he would continue to think of it as long as it stood.

Nor was its enormous size the only remarkable thing about it. The young eaglets were standing erect on the huge platform, and for the first time in his life Dave Barrows was looking at three fledgling eagles in a single brood.

He used his binoculars to make sure. "I know it happens," he said finally to Reino, "but I never expected to see it. I doubt that one eagle nest in five hundred raises three young."

They went on to the rim of the cliff, followed the narrow shelf down to the pine, and Barrows made ready for the climb.

He had no dread of it. His leg irons were the high-rigger kind, worn by the men who topped towering trees for spars in west-coast logging operations. The spurs, almost five inches long and sharp as awls, were beveled to pierce through the thickest bark and find a secure hold in the wood of any tree.

The tall pine, with its straight smooth trunk leaning slightly in toward the cliff, free of branches all the way to the fork that held the nest, offered no obstacles. Nevertheless, it measured well over four feet across on the stump. A climb of eighty feet up a tree of that size is a dizzying thing for an onlooker to watch, and the man who undertakes it must be watchful and alert at every step.

Barrows buckled on the irons and hung a coil of line at his belt. Next he snapped two safety ropes into the wider leather belt he wore low on his hips, flipped one around the trunk of the pine, adjusted it for length, drove the spurs deep into green wood, and began the ascent.

He climbed as a lineman goes up a utility pole, leaning back into the loop of rope, well away from the tree, his weight resting on the spurs, taking one sure step after another. When he reached the fork of the pine the second rope would be thrown over it and made fast before he unsnapped the first. In that manner he would be roped to the tree or its branches at all times. From the nest, he would lower the coil of line and pull up his cameras. It was a routine familiar to him.

He reached the fork, climbed around it without difficulty, and went up another dozen feet. When his head came level with the rim of the nest the three eaglets, alerted by the noise of his ascent, were crouched on the far side of the platform, hissing in fear and resentment.

He went higher, until he was standing on the side of the nest, roped securely to a vertical branch half as thick as his own body. In that instant a shadow fell across the tree, and before he could look up he heard and felt a rush of air in his face as one of the adult eagles swooped past, hardly more than the reach of his arm overhead.

He had given no real thought to the old birds while he made the climb. They had behaved as all their kind he had encountered always did, soaring in wide circles across the sky, screaming in anger at his intrusion, but never coming within a hundred yards of the nest. Barrows told himself that they must regard it as a place of great danger. In his years of bird work he had neither known nor read of eagles behaving differently. Owls sometimes attacked savagely if their nest was invaded, and less often hawks did the same thing. But not eagles.

As that broad shadow passed over him and the wing-stirred

wind struck his face, Dave Barrows realized that he was dealing with an unheard of and dangerous situation. If the eagle—he guessed it to be the female—pressed home her attack, she was capable of dealing severe injuries. He was fast to the pine and in no danger of falling, but he had no way to protect his face and head, and he knew that those mailed talons could break the neck of a full-grown deer.

There was no chance to retreat. With a curious, half-detached feeling of helplessness, he looked up and waited to see what would happen next.

The eagle climbed steeply until she was fifty feet above him. There she turned in a tight wingover and came slanting down once more.

She did not scream or squeal, and the very silence of the attack made it all the more ominous. But when she was less than a couple of yards away, she swerved and did as she had done before, knifing harmlessly over with a rush of air that sounded like a strong wind in the pine top. That time Barrows had a clear glimpse of her down-thrust feet, the great talons spread as if reaching for quarry the bird did not quite dare to strike, and he felt a sharp surge of relief when she was past.

She climbed again, a dozen yards above the highest branches of the pine. Then she tilted into an almost vertical stoop, falling with the speed of a stone, straight for the man's upturned face.

There was no way to fend that attack. He flattened against the branch that secured him and in the fleeting two or three seconds of her arrowing dive he had time only to throw up a free arm to protect his head.

The eagle braked when she was so close that the air trapped in her cupped wings made a sound like a muffled explosion. Again Barrows had a clear look at those terrible mailed feet, close enough to touch, and a wingtip brushed his hair. Then she was gone, as swiftly and silently as she had first come. Within a minute she had joined her mate that was still circling over the lake and ridges, and the troubled screaming of the two of them was an angry duet once more.

When his heart stopped pounding, the man lowered himself onto his knees on the nest, drew the eaglets to him one at a time and fitted them with the numbered aluminum leg bands they would wear the rest of their days. He banded the big male fledgling last of all, and the bird submitted, hissing in protest. Not again in all the years of his life would this proud young eagle know the touch of human hands.

"One of those eaglets is marked with white—unlike any eagle of his kind I ever saw," Barrows told his friend as he stepped away from the trunk of the pine and bent to unbuckle his irons. "He reminds me of the sea eagle from Kamchatka that I saw on my trip to Alaska ten years ago. It had wandered east across the Bering Sea as a stray and injured a wing somehow. Hal Berndt at the university was nursing it back to health in a cage. It was a splendid thing, big and powerful and fierce, refusing to be tamed, and its brown-and-white plumage made it more striking than any American eagle I have seen. Berndt had named it the Sky Khan.

"I guess that would be a good name for this youngster," he went on. "He's marked much the same way."

That was how the pied eagle came by the name by which Dave Barrows would call him the rest of his life. Khan.

"He'd be easy to keep track of if he stayed around," Dave told Tormala, "but once he takes flight I don't suppose we'll ever see him again."

Barrows was wrong. He would see the white-marked eagle many times, but not until five years had passed would their acquaintance be renewed.

Before he left the place that day, Barrows made a decision that was to influence his life for the next quarter century.

Less than a hundred feet along the rim of the escarpment from the aerie tree was another ancient pine, a Norway of about equal size but with branches sprawling out from its trunk, from

a point thirty feet above the ground all the way to the top. Because it grew on the rim, while the aerie pine was rooted on a
ledge twenty feet lower down, the green crown of the Norway
brushed the sky at a higher level than that of the other tree. The
tops of the two were no more than twenty-five yards apart, with
open space between.

Barrows studied the situation carefully, walking around the
sturdy, rough-barked trunk of the Norway.

"I think I've found something I have been looking for," he
said at last. "There has to be room up in those branches some-
where for a platform and a tree blind that will look down into
the nest at easy camera range. If I'm right, this is my chance to
watch and photograph the life of a family of eagles. It's something I've wanted to do for years."

He buckled his irons back in place, went up the Norway to
the first branches and climbed easily the rest of the way. At a
level a dozen feet higher than the top of the eagle nest in the
neighboring pine, he found what he sought: two stout branches
that forked away from the trunk horizontally, a perfect support
for the platform he had in mind.

Three days later he and Reino came back. They parked
their station wagon on the road that ran along the Lake Superior
shore and packed what they needed across the ridges to the
escarpment rim.

The boards for the platform had been carefully measured
and precut. It would be five feet square, with a rim a few inches
high on all sides to prevent equipment from sliding off. Dave
toted the bundle of lumber; his partner carried two lengths of
two-by-fours that would serve as beams to support the structure.
The tools they divided between them.

They stopped at the foot of the last terrace before they
climbed to the top of the escarpment, so as not to disturb the
eagles, and nailed the platform together. At the Norway Dave
went up to the two branches he had chosen, lowered a coil of
line, drew up the two-by-fours, and spiked them in place. The

platform was hauled up next and nailed to the beams. Then Tormala knotted onto the line four small poles, cut and trimmed on the spot, that would form a frame for a low tent of faded green burlap. Last, the tent was hung in place, and the job was done.

The blind had room enough for a man to sit or kneel in its cramped floor space. He could even curl up and catch snatches of sleep there. The small tent was too low to allow him to stand erect, but there would be no reason to do that.

Most important, when the work was finished the structure was not conspicuous among the green branches of the pine. Barrows studied it from the ground with satisfaction. There was nothing about it to alarm the eagles. He would give them three or four days to forget that the men had been here.

When he came back again he came in full darkness, two hours before daybreak, with one of his graduate students, hiking to the place with flashlights over a route that was now becoming familiar. Before they were within sight of the nest they extinguished the lights and finished the walk in complete silence. They strapped on their irons, and Barrows sent his helper up to the platform first. When he was safely perched on it, and the coil of line came snaking down, Dave tied on the cameras, and as soon as they had vanished into the burlap tent overhead he climbed up.

When daybreak began to brighten in the east, an hour later, and the she eagle soared away from the nest, the two men were watching through a small aperture in the burlap, their presence in the neighboring tree totally unsuspected by the eagles. Dave Barrows had exactly what he had wanted, a lookout post close to an eagle nest, and a very extraordinary nest in the bargain. Taking its huge size into account, plus the fact that it sheltered three eaglets rather than one or two, and that one of them bore strange markings that would serve to identify him wherever he went as long as he lived, the whole situation was nothing short of ideal.

But now there had been a change. There were no longer three fledgling birds in the nest. One was missing.

When the two men quitted the blind in midafternoon, they followed the narrow ledge down to the saucer-shaped shelf where the aerie pine grew, and there they found the smallest of the three eaglets, battered and trampled into a shapeless lump of bone and flesh and feathers.

It had happened the day after the blind was put up. The eaglets awakened at daybreak, stretched and voided, and looked around the flattened platform of the nest. A big sucker lay there untouched, the last food brought by the parents before dusk the night before.

The older of the two females, most aggressive of the brood, pounced on it, tore out the gills and swallowed them, and began to rip open the belly of the fish. It was the misfortune of the youngest eaglet just then to challenge her brood mate for the food. Crazed with hunger, she leaped at the sucker, seized it in her bill and undertook to drag it away.

There was a brief tug-of-war, and then the bigger eaglet, four days older and more fierce as well as stronger, turned on her in blind rage, buffeting her with wings and beak, striking savagely with mailed feet already capable of tearing a three-pound fish open with a single stroke. The younger eagle went down under the first blows and did not regain her feet. The attack was to the death, and it was over within minutes. While it lasted, the white-marked male eaglet stood on the opposite rim of the nest, watching with complete detachment.

The parent eagles came back, one by one, but they paid no attention to the dead fledgling. She lay on the dry grass of the platform for three days, until she was trod upon, sodden from rain, hardly recognizable for what she was. Then the adult she eagle dropped her over the rim to the ground, where Barrows found her.

3

FLIGHT

Dave Barrows went back to the blind often during the remaining days of June, sometimes with a companion, sometimes alone. Each time he climbed in darkness to avoid alerting the eagles. For the most part that ruse succeeded, but a couple of times as he began his ascent of the Norway he heard the wing clatter of one of the old birds leaving the nest and realized that they were aware of him despite the cover of darkness.

He would have found it difficult to explain the fascination these majestic birds held for him.

In part it was because of their wild and regal ways. They resented and feared man with a fierce intensity. Lovers of wilderness and solitude, like all their kind, they nested and reared their cruel-eyed young in deep forest where man rarely intruded.

And because of that aloofness, humans did not often have a chance to spy on their family life as Barrows was doing now, and that added to his enjoyment of the opportunity.

As a youngster, he had been intrigued by stories of eagles carrying children away to their nests. He had wondered what such a dreadful fate would be like. How would the huge nest look? What would the feelings of the victim be when the birds pounced on him for the kill?

Now he set such tales down as no more than the product of lively imagination. He had found, in all the literature of birds, no authenticated instance of eagles carrying children off, although on a very few occasions they had swooped down and attacked a small child, clutching and tearing its clothing, probably in the mistaken belief that it was other prey.

But at least he was getting the answers to the questions he had asked himself as a young boy. He knew exactly what an eagle aerie looked like, how the old birds brought in their prey, and how the fledglings tore at it and fed, and he was finding the knowledge curiously satisfying.

The two young birds in the Great Nest were at the peak of their flight training now. They awakened before full daylight each morning and the parent that had kept watch over them through the night left at once, to hunt.

The two fledglings stretched, relieved themselves carefully without soiling more than the rim of the nest, opened and tested the wings that had almost the spread of a full-grown eagle's. Next they walked about the big platform, and often one or the other selected a loose stick two or three feet long, picked it up in bill or talons and carried or tossed it to a new location.

Usually it was not long after daylight before one or the other of the old eagles came to the nest with food, most often a freshly taken fish still wet and glistening in the level rays of the rising sun.

The eaglets needed no help with such prey now. The parent dropped it and they seized it, tore it open and began to feed. The old eagle left at once to resume hunting. When the eaglets had finished their meal they rested briefly, and then one at a time they walked to the rim of the nest, balanced there a

moment, stretched their wings, and launched themselves into the air in a series of stiff jumps. At each leap they rose higher, lifting with strong wingbeats, until they were springing almost to the height of a man's head, their yellow feet dangling so that they bore a ridiculous resemblance to a small boy lofting himself into the air with his pants hanging down.

On windy days, when the top of the pine swayed back and forth, carrying the nest with it, it seemed time and again that they would miss it in landing or be carried beyond the rim by the wind. But their sense of balance in the air was faultless now and they had sufficient strength in their great wings to control their abortive flights as precisely as adult birds. Watching them, alternately marveling at their skill and chuckling at their antics, Dave Barrows was convinced that they were fully capable of flight many days before they finally chose to quit the nest.

That happened on a warm morning in July, after a hard thunderstorm had rolled across the Sleeping Bears at daybreak. That morning he had delayed his climb to the blind until the storm was over. He went up in full light, but the eagle family seemed to have grown used to him now and once he was hidden in the tiny tent they paid him no further attention.

The morning stayed windy, and both the aerie pine and the Norway swung in wide arcs. In midmorning one of the old eagles—Barrows took it to be the female since it was the larger of the pair—came to the nest with a fish but did not alight. Instead she sailed past fifteen or twenty feet away, circled and repeated her flight, while the hungry eaglets crouched and watched her, squealing loudly to make known their hunger.

But the old bird refused to go to them. She circled the nest three or four times, and suddenly the smaller of the young launched herself into the air with a powerful leap and hung above the nest, hovering and pleading to be fed. The parent bird swept close now, no more than a wing length away, with a series of wild and taunting screams, and suddenly the fledgling followed her with strong wing strokes, as if to overtake her and wrest the fish away. Within seconds the eaglet was in full flight.

Back in the nest the white-marked male stood watching briefly as his nest mate, his parent, and his breakfast receded over the first ridge. Half a mile away the old bird alighted on a dead tree and surrendered the fish, and the fledgling female fed.

In that instant Khan leaped off the nest and the swaying of the pine carried it out from beneath him, so that he had open space under his wings. He rose higher, breasting the wind, at home finally in the element he had been born to, and flew toward the tree where the second fledgling was tearing at her fish.

Dave watched him go with a strange lifting of the heart. This was the moment he had waited for and hoped to witness, from the day of his first visit to the Great Nest.

"So long and good luck, Khan," he murmured. "I don't suppose I'll ever see you again, but I hope that band I gave you is a long time turning up."

Khan had been more than a fortnight on the wing when he made his first kill. Up to that time he had subsisted chiefly on the bounty his parents brought to him, although a couple of times he had found freshly dead fish cast up on the Lake Superior beach and had feasted on his own.

There came a morning when he was hunting above the small lake just downstream from the falls on the Laughing Whitefish. He had been hungry for two days now, finding no food of his own and forced to fast because the old eagles were tapering off their care of the two grown fledglings.

At that moment a small school of suckers lay basking near the top of the water, where the river ran out of the lake, deep and slow-currented because of a series of beaver dams. From half a thousand feet overhead, the eyes of the cruising young eagle made them out and he slanted down like a speeding dark arrow.

It was an easy kill. Too late the suckers saw the diving bird. They scattered and submerged in a flurry of water. But Khan struck with a loud splash, and his feet reached under and found the smooth round back of a fish. The talons of both feet locked like steel hooks, and he flapped up and rose easily into the air.

A quarter mile away, along the shore of the lake, a dead pine leaned over the water. He flew to it, found a secure perch, and fed greedily.

Twice on that short flight, he had sent a wild scream of triumph and delight ringing out across the timbered ridges. He did not comprehend his own feelings, did not even understand the meaning of those fierce cries.

He was celebrating a rite, the ancestral raptor ritual of killing that he would honor each day as long as he lived, in part because of the endless goad of hunger, in part because the urge to hunt and kill ran in his very blood, was an essential part of his joy at being alive.

All his life would be marked by violent killing, as he had killed the unwary sucker. To kill was to feed, to fail was to go hungry. But there was also the fierce delight of combat and the elation of victory that had been bred into his kind for as long as eagles had cruised the sky. He had been born a monarch of the air lanes, but his reign would be neither gentle nor merciful. In his world, combat meant death for the one that lost. He would deal it as casually as a robin gleaning earthworms on a lawn, and when his own turn finally came he would meet it with beak and claw and accept it without quailing, as part of the natural law by which he had lived. He would die tearing at whatever threatened him, sustained by battle rage and knowing no fear.

As long as he lived he would prefer fish to any other food. But in the press of hunger he would take birds almost as readily, and because he would never hunt far from water, they would be for the most part water birds, ducks, herons, gulls, occasionally even loons or geese that weighed more than he did.

Now and then, too, urged by a strange inner command, he would stoop on and kill some creature that wore fur instead of feathers, and revel in the warm red flesh.

The two young eagles came back to the Great Nest many times that summer, to roost on or near it with their parents. But as the year began to wane and the first stirrings of the urge to migrate awoke in them with the approach of autumn, they ranged farther and farther away and returned less often. In the end they severed completely their ties with the natal aerie, ready to take up the fiercely independent lives of adult eagles. The young female did not live to begin her first flight south.

On a bright October day, when autumn haze lay like smoke over the tumbled ridges of the Sleeping Bears and Siskowet Lake was a blue patch on an incredible flaming tapestry of red and gold, she was hunting above the lower reaches of the Laughing Whitefish when she saw a small animal move slowly across a fire-created opening on the riverbank below her.

She came down swiftly, in a tight spiral. Two hundred feet above the treetops she checked her descent and hung almost motionless in the windless air, wanting a closer look.

The thing on the ground was the size of a small woodchuck, bigger than the squirrel she had killed only a few days before, but not too big to serve her as prey. It was grizzled in black and white and it walked with an awkward, waddling gait.

An older eagle would have known not to attack this queer, slothful creature except under the press of starvation. Everything about it—its size, color, purposeless way of walking—flashed a warning that the meat eaters of the wilderness had learned to heed over a thousand generations. But the young eagle was not yet attuned to such inborn warnings.

A bleached log thrust out from the shore of the river into the dark deep water. The porcupine, itself not more than half grown, came to the upturned roots of the log, clambered up and walked slowly out along the trunk. When it reached the end it stopped, testing the water with first one forefoot and then the other, trying to make up its slow-witted mind whether to swim the river or turn back.

In that instant the eagle decided to kill. She fell in a steep stoop and struck hard, locking her feet deep in the back of her victim. She bent her head to tear at the nape of its neck. And then she felt the burning, stabbing pain in her legs, her breast, her throat. Even in one eye.

When she wrenched free and lifted toward the sky again, she left the porcupine mortally hurt behind her. But in turn she carried more than a hundred of its quills bedded deep in her flesh.

Some she had self-impaled with the force of her strike. Others, including those in her throat and eye, the porcupine had driven home with quick flailing strokes of its tail.

The tips of those quills each bore a thousand tiny barbs, too small for the naked eye to see but deadly as the barbs of an arrowhead. They could not be plucked out. Every movement the bird made would only serve to pull them deeper until they came to rest against solid bone.

She could not know it, but she had paid the penalty that has to be paid by almost every flesh eater of the wilderness that ventures to launch itself at the quilled dolt. Most know better, but there is hardly one, from fox to wolf and from owl to eagle, that does not make the mistake from time to time and forfeit its life. Even predators as lordly as the tiger and lion die a sorry death now and then from the long quills of an Asian or African porcupine sunk in their vitals.

There is in the woods of North America one wild hunter exempt from the consequences of an attack on the quill-armed sloth. That is the fisher, next of kin to weasel, marten, and mink. It singles out the porcupine as a favorite prey, kills it by flipping it on its back and tearing open the unprotected underbelly, and eats the flesh out of the skin as one would lick empty a paper bag. Even if the fisher picks up a few quills with its meal they do not penetrate its flesh, for reasons human beings do not understand.

Although it took the young eagle two weeks to die, and her death was painful every hour, she did not hunt again.

At first she perched in a tree she had used many times, and tried to pull the quills from her legs and breast with her beak. A few came free, but most of them were sunk too deep in muscle for the barbs to give way.

The eagle stayed in the tree for most of three days, sick and moping, blinded on one side, burning agony running through all her body. Slowly but inexorably the quills festered and worked deeper, in throat and belly, tongue and even the roof of her mouth. When they reached vital organs they would kill her, unless she died of hunger first.

The urge to find food and water drove her at last back to the shore of the river. But there was no food to be found, and she lifted painfully and flew on to the Lake Superior beach.

There for another week she walked a slow patrol, growing steadily more weak and wretched.

In the end she found shelter of a sort beneath the trunk of a fallen tree at the edge of the beach, and there she lived out the last three days of her life, earthbound, bedraggled, and inglorious, the will to live growing more and more dim. On a night of cold wind and autumn rain that turned to sleet and wet snow toward morning, death finally put an end to her ordeal.

Khan spent his first winter on the shores of a sprawling man-made lake in the mountains of Tennessee, a thousand miles from the Great Nest. Fish and ducks were plentiful in and around that mountain lake, and by the time he began the leisurely fall flight south he had become a skilled hunter. He fared well.

Close to the end of winter he started back to the vicinity of the nest where he had been born, but the old eagles were there ahead of him and they would not brook his presence.

The male drove him off with angry screams, in all likelihood unaware that he was threatening his own son. The adult birds were busy now with their springtime affairs—courting, mating, repairing the nest—and they wanted no intruder to come near. At the end of a week of harassment Khan gave up, drifted away, and took up his life of adolescent bachelorhood along a river that offered him food for the taking. He would not see either of his parents again.

THE SUCCESSION

Khan was approaching his third spring, still in the brown plumage of his youth and feeling as yet no urge to seek a mate, when the change came at the Great Nest. He was hunting along a river five hundred miles away, drifting slowly north to his summer country, on the day it happened.

The two eagles that had sired and brooded and reared him returned to the aerie early that year, while February snow still lay deep in the Sleeping Bears. Food was scarce.

The winter had been hard, and except in the rapids there was no open water the length of the Laughing Whitefish, no place for winter ducks to feed and loiter. A field of rough ice, veined with pressure ridges, had built twenty miles out into Lake Superior, making it fruitless to hunt the shore.

The eagles sought prey in the timber, hunting like overgrown hawks, and picked up a grouse or squirrel often enough to fend off starvation. But many days they went hungry. Twice a solitary gull came wandering across the ice field from the distant open lake, and both times the bird was struck down the instant it came within sight. In such ways they eked out a lean living, waiting for the spring breakup.

On a day in early March a flock of a dozen wild geese entered their hunting territory, flying north to muskeg nesting grounds along the shores of James Bay, marshes that were still locked in ice and snow. As for all their kind that ventured north ahead of spring, this advance-guard flock faced severe risks. Impelled to migrate by inborn urges they themselves did not comprehend, urges triggered by the increasing hours of daylight, they would arrive in the harsh land that was their summer home at a time when late-winter storms would still beset them and feeding places would be hard to find, even on the muddy tide flats of the sea itself.

They came over the Sleeping Bears in their usual flight formation, driving a living wedge across the spring sky, led by an air-wise old gander that had made the spring journey a dozen times and knew the way to the flock's destination by unfailing instincts that men will never fathom. They flew steadily northward, crying in resonant voices as they went. When the male eagle first took note of their approach they had come three hundred miles since daybreak. They would rest that night on a river to the north of Lake Superior, in a place the old gander remembered well.

The eagle saw them, watched their steady flight until they were abreast of him, only a mile away. He launched himself from his lookout perch and, like a streaking brown missile, drove after them in savage pursuit.

The geese saw him coming and their measured flight talk changed to a wild clamor of alarm. Their wingbeats quickened in panic, and the leader veered off on a new course, hoping to take them beyond the reach of the fierce raptor that was following them.

There was no chance of that. A wild Canada goose, unmolested, flies between forty-five and fifty miles an hour. Under the press of terror, he can build that to close to sixty miles. The eagle bearing down on the flock now was overhauling them as a greyhound runs down a jackrabbit. Humans have never clocked the flight speed of an attacking eagle, and probably will never be able to, but it is almost beyond belief for the short distance needed. No bird that kills in the air, not even the great falcons, can outdistance the bald eagle in straight flight.

A mile out over the ice the eagle overtook his prey. A young goose, making her first flight north and tired from long hours on the wing, lagged behind the rest at the last minute, and it was she that he chose.

He did not stoop on her from above, as a falcon would have done. Instead he came up behind her in level flight, and at the last instant he rolled in the air, flashed under her with his back to the earth, reached up, and sank his talons in her breast and belly.

Those great feet had almost the spread of a man's hand, and the muscles and tendons that closed their curved claws had the strength of steel springs. The stricken goose faltered and started to fall, and was dead before she struck the ice below.

The eagle kept his grip in her flesh, but made no effort to carry her off. Her weight was little more than half of his, and he was easily capable of supporting it, but he did not try. Instead he fell with her, braking the descent with his wings, and tumbled down to a landing. Once on the ice he tore and began to eat.

His mate, cruising in wide circles over the Sleeping Bears, saw the kill and slanted toward him. She alighted on the ice close by, walked to him and was welcomed. They fed together.

The goose provided the best meal they had had in many days. When it was gone, hunger stalked them again. A March blizzard swept in off Lake Superior, deepening the snow in the mountains, and while it lasted even the grouse and squirrels stayed in their places of shelter.

It was almost a week after the goose kill when the female, patrolling the ridges between the Great Nest and the Superior beach on a morning of intense cold, took note of a little band of ravens in the timber below.

Half of them were clustered in a knot around some darkish object in the snow; the rest were perched in nearby trees. She dropped instantly to investigate.

Renegade dogs, a mixed pack of hounds and collies and curs recruited from the farming country to the south of the mountains, had drifted north a few weeks before, running and killing deer as they went, blood-hungry and merciless as wolves.

They had found a small yard, covering three or four acres, on a hemlock ridge along the Laughing Whitefish. A dozen deer were wintering there and the ridge was laced with their hard-packed runways. Driven off those paths into the belly-deep soft snow on either side, the animals were almost as easily overtaken as domestic sheep. The renegades killed four in a single night, ate their fill, drove a young doe heavy with fawn out beyond the border of the yard and ran her for the sport of it.

They caught her quickly, on the ridge where the ravens were now gathered, and tore her belly open as she ran, so that her entrails dragged in the snow. When she stumbled and went down they worried her, left her to die, and went their way, making a big circle back toward the farmyards and firesides that were their homes.

Days later a bounty trapper named Nunn had found the frozen carcass of the doe and set three steel traps around it, not expecting the dogs to return but in the hope that coyotes or a bobcat might pay a visit as the snow settled in the March sun.

Now ravens had found the deer and were making their usual use of it.

The eagle alighted close beside the feeding scavengers. They scattered and hopped away, but did not take flight. They had shared meals of this kind with eagles times enough to know that they were in no danger so long as they did not challenge the claim of the bigger bird.

She walked in toward the deer, and the ravens gave more ground. She was two steps from the torn belly of the doe when the steel jaws of a trap snapped shut on her leg just above the foot. Bone crunched and pain knifed deep into her. She leaped into the air, but the trap chain checked her and she tumbled down again.

She fought the trap unceasingly for hours, until exhaustion left her huddled on the snow with half-spread wings, only the movements of her fierce yellow eyes revealing that she still lived. The ravens had watched her struggles from their perches in small trees nearby. When she lay quiet, they flew down to the deer, careful only to keep beyond her reach, and resumed picking at the frozen meat. They were the only witnesses to the eagle's death.

In milder weather her agony might have been prolonged for days, until exhaustion and hunger and thirst finished her. The bitter cold of the March nights was more merciful. On the second morning she lay still and frozen in the snow beside the dead deer. The feeding ravens no longer paid her the slightest attention.

It was there Dave Barrows found her. He was on his way in to the Great Nest, on snowshoes and alone, checking to learn whether the eagles had returned. Halfway up the last ridge below the escarpment that overlooked Siskowet Lake, he saw ravens wheeling above the trees a hundred yards away, and turned aside to investigate.

He cursed fervently at what he found, took the frozen bird from the trap and went on. He would carry her back to serve as a study skin.

He waited half an hour in the vicinity of the aerie, hidden in a clump of low evergreens, before he saw a solitary eagle sweeping the sky in wide circles. While he watched, it spiraled down, alighted on the rim of the Great Nest and stood for a long time, a desolate and lonely figure, searching the blue vault overhead, plainly waiting for another of its kind to appear.

Barrows knew then, as surely as if the actors in the drama

had left written records, what had happened. The pair of eagles he had spied on for three seasons, mated for life like all their kind, was broken now. The crumpled frozen female he had removed from the trap was the she eagle from this nest. The bereft male perched now on its rim was the survivor of the pair.

What would happen next Dave could only guess. He knew that mated eagles, although staunchly loyal through all their lifetimes, were quick to remate if one of the pair was lost. Would this male seek and find a second female and bring her here to the aerie with him, to carry on the family dynasty he had founded almost a decade earlier? Or would he abandon the place and search elsewhere for a mate and the site of a new nest? There was no way to foretell.

The male eagle spent most of a fortnight circling and hunting above the Sleeping Bears, voicing his aloneness at times with fierce screaming. Now and then he came down to perch on the rim of the nest, a forlorn thing robbed of all that the season should have brought him, watching the distant ridges for another of his own kind.

On a crisp morning in late March it happened. He saw the strange eagle as a speck in the sky, too small with distance for human eyes to make out. He tipped instantly off the aerie and flew to meet the newcomer.

She was a young female, approaching her fourth summer, and although she still wore the brown plumage of her adolescence she was ready to mate.

The old eagle courted her with the ardent nuptial flight of his kind, circling, spiraling and screaming. In the end he led her down to the Great Nest, claimed her and left his seed in her. Three days later Barrows saw the two of them repairing the aerie and he knew what had happened. Probably not more often than once in hundreds of times, he knew, did a mature eagle mate with a young bird still in brown plumage.

That pairing would last only through two seasons, and in each of those years the she eagle would produce a single fledgling.

Late in the second autumn, when the two were nearly ready to quit the Sleeping Bear country for the winter, the male bird alighted one morning in a dead tree at the mouth of the Laughing Whitefish and sat preening.

At that moment, fifty yards upriver, an outlaw trapper was making a set where an otter slide went steeply down the bank into the water.

Bill Nunn had drifted north a few years before from the backwoods of the southern mountains, coming as a woodcutter, and had taken up at once the life of lawlessness he had left behind in the mountain cove where he had been born.

He killed deer when it pleased him, shining them with a jacklight in summer and early fall, following them into their yards on snowshoes in winter, using the haunches and leaving the rest for the ravens and other wild scavengers. He trapped coyotes and bobcats, and now and then a stray timber wolf, for the bounty money. But his main source of income was illegal beaver trapping.

Twenty years earlier, persistent poaching had all but exterminated the beaver population of the Lake Superior country. But given protection and more diligent enforcement of the laws that safeguarded them, the animals had built up in numbers with the rapidity that is characteristic of all rodents, so that now virtually every small stream had its beaver dam and pond, and the big mud-and-stick houses lifted their rounded domes along the banks of many of the larger rivers.

There was a short open season in March and early April of each year, when trappers were allowed to take a limited number of pelts. But the ice had not yet gone out of the ponds and creeks at that time, and woods roads were still blocked with snow, so that trapping was difficult and not too productive. Bill Nunn did not bother with it.

Instead, he began his beaver harvest in November, followed his trapline until the ice came, and then waited for the spring breakup before he resumed. He trapped as long as the skins stayed prime, until some time in May, and his total take each year was many times the legal quota allowed under the law. Now and then, too, he came across otter sign and took two or three dark, lustrous pelts that fetched double the price of the finest beaver.

Only a week or two before, Nunn had had word from Baldy Vachon, keeper of the ramshackle general store at the hamlet of Pine Stump, where he disposed of his contraband catch. Vachon had told him there was now a market for eagle plumes.

"Indians want 'em for their powwows," Baldy explained. "War bonnets, medicine sticks, and the like. It's against the law to shoot eagles, and they're hard to get. I can pay you $20 for a good pair of wings."

It was modest bait. Vachon himself had been promised double that by a professional plume buyer eager to supply the illegal traffic. But it was bait enough to launch Bill Nunn on a career of eagle hunting that would combine nicely with the rest of his outlaw activities.

He saw the male eagle alight in the tree within easy rifle range, and instantly he reached a cautious hand for the work-worn .30–30 leaning against a log beside him.

The bird was a regal-looking creature, with his snow-white head and tail, great yellow feet clutching a branch, golden eyes made more fierce by the beetling brows that shadowed them. But the poacher wasted no time in admiration. He laid the rifle against the trunk of a convenient aspen and squeezed the trigger.

The heavy slug smashed the eagle in the breast and knocked him backward from his perch. He was dead when he struck the ground. Nunn walked to him, glanced at the stain of blood spreading down his body. Then he pulled free the white tail plumes, severed both wings with deft knife strokes, and slipped into the cover of nearby undergrowth.

On a sunny morning when winter was coming to an end in

the Sleeping Bears, Dave Barrows found the two eagles working at their annual task of nest repair. But to his astonishment, in addition to the normal white head and tail, one bore the strange white markings he had first seen in the plumage of the eaglet he had banded at that same aerie five springs before.

Khan had come back—a proud young king in the full plumage of an adult eagle. Khan had returned to claim the Great Nest for his own.

THE WINTER FLIGHT

The young female that had served Khan's father as a mate for two summers had flown south by herself after Nunn shot the male, and begun a winter of erratic wandering.

In a country of rough, wooded bluffs along a big Kentucky river she had found a gathering of a dozen of her own kind, and had tarried there for a month. But she was driven by a queer restlessness, perhaps because she was no longer a mated bird, and in the end she drifted on to the southeast until she came to a place in the north of Florida where there were many lakes, and where rivers wound between timbered hills.

To an eagle accustomed and attuned to the northern wilderness, this was an alien land: a country of live oaks whose Spanish moss hung in long silver gray streamers, pine flatwoods with thick ground cover of vines and palmetto hammocks, and blackwater cypress swamps strewn with dead trees. In all her brief years the young eagle had found no hunting ground like it.

The lakes and rivers teemed with her favorite food—bass, sunfish, suckers, catfish, gar, and grindel. Ducks and coots, grebes and gallinules came here to winter by the thousands, migrating from their northern nesting grounds. There were small herons to be had for the killing, and doves in the uplands. Rabbits were everywhere, both cottontails and their next of kin, the marsh rabbits—the canecutters of human hunters—that weighed twice as much. In this land of plenty, hunting was almost effortless.

The day the eagle arrived, tired and hungry from flight, she saw a thick-bodied grindel lying just under the surface of a swampy lake. She hovered briefly over it, plunged, and set her talons in its back. It was more than she wanted for a meal, but she alighted in a nearby cypress and fed to repletion, letting the rest of the mangled fish drop to the ground when she was finished.

The next morning, perched on a dead pine snag, she watched for a long time a scene that had not changed since the moccasins of the long-forgotten Apalachee Indians had whispered on the riverbank trails of the region four centuries before.

Directly before her, a live-oak ridge sloped down to the border of a flooded swamp where turtles sunned themselves on rotting mossy logs and where, in summer, thick-bodied water moccasins shared the logs or slithered through the saw grass. On the bank, of no interest to the eagle, a six-foot-long alligator lay sprawled on the black mud.

Doves and brown thrashers moved through the trees around the motionless eagle, quail called from a nearby opening in the pine woods, and on a ridge across the swamp a wild gobbler set the woods ringing with loud yelping cries. A cottontail rabbit hopped across a clear place on the ground directly below the dead pine, but the eagle was not hungry and she paid no attention.

She could also see from her perch a diamondback rattlesnake as long as the height of a tall man, basking in the pale winter sun on a mound of sand at the entrance of a den. It lay relaxed and unmoving, like a coil of very thick rope, flat head resting on the body, the rattles still. But for all its harmless appearance death lurked in those coils, and by instinct the eagle wanted no part of the snake.

What she could not know was that the diamondback shared its den with a strange companion. The burrow had been dug by a gopher tortoise, a big land turtle more than a foot long, and it went back into the ground for thirty feet, a fairly straight tunnel that slanted three or four feet below the surface. The tortoise had pushed the earth out and heaped it in a low mound, where the snake lay now, so that the burrow looked like the den of a groundhog or badger, save that in cross section it was not round. The gopher had dug it in the form of a half circle, to fit his own high, rounded shell, with a flat floor, so that it was shaped like the door of a primitive oven.

At the inner end of the burrow there was a roomy chamber. In that dark, cool retreat the tortoise, shy and retiring by nature and also disliking the heat of the sun, spent most of the daylight hours. At night he wandered out, to feed but not to hunt, for he was a vegetarian, placidly content with grass and foliage. Here, too, he passed the winters, chiefly in retirement.

Like a great majority of the gopher tortoises of north Florida, this one shared his quarters winter and summer with the big diamondback that lay basking now at the entrance to the tunnel. Like the tortoise, the snake hunted by night and rested in the inner chamber of the den by day. His kind did not hibernate, as snakes do in the north, but with the approach of winter he retreated into the burrow and became inactive until the warming days of March called him out once more.

The relationship between snake and tortoise was one of the strangest in the outdoor world. The tortoise held no interest for the rattler as prey, and it did not regard him as an enemy. They shared their lightless retreat in complete harmony, neither one posing a threat to the other.

The eagle had perched motionless on the dead snag for more than an hour, scanning with casual interest the ridge and the swamp at its foot, when the alligator suddenly stirred. It lifted its thick body on short stout legs, slid noiselessly into the dark water of the swamp, submerged, and vanished among the cypress knees and rotting logs. The eagle turned her head and watched it go, knowing that in her world any movement or change of situation had meaning.

Minutes later four wood drakes lifted out of the swamp, quacking in alarm, and arrowed away above the treetops. The little band had numbered five, but the gator, coming up soundlessly beneath them, had crushed one in great jaws that snapped shut like a steel trap.

The eagle was not yet genuinely hungry, but the sight of the four ducks in panic-stricken flight triggered the fierce hunting instinct that lay always at the surface of her life. Her eyes kindled with the lust to kill and she tipped from her perch and gave chase.

She overtook the ducks as a goshawk overtakes a fleeing grouse. Already frightened by the attack of the alligator, they separated and fled at the fastest flight speed they could attain.

But it did them no good.

The eagle singled out a young drake, overhauled him, and sent him diving headlong toward the ground. Before he could gain the shelter of the treetops she clutched and killed him. She swept up with the prey in her talons, looked for and found a perch that suited her, landed, and fed.

In the territory where she hunted there were three mated pairs of eagles, the southern race of her kind, so like her that professional ornithologists found it difficult to distinguish one from the other.

When she first encountered them, they tolerated her. But because of the mild and snow-free winters of Florida, their nesting season was far earlier than hers. In December, shortly after she arrived in their land of plenty, they began to repair their nests.

There were other reasons for the early nesting, too, built into the behavior pattern of the southern eagles over thousands of years. Winter, when waterfowl are most abundant, is the time when the old birds can feed the fledglings most easily. And by the time the heat of summer arrives, the young are either out of the nest or old enough to endure it.

In January, when the nests of all three pairs held eggs, their attitude toward the stranger from the north underwent a change. She suddenly became an interloper in their nesting territory, and if her hunting took her near an aerie one or the other of the owners drove her off with angry screams. She tolerated this hostility for only a few days. When one of the southern males launched an especially determined attack on her one morning, she climbed swiftly to elude him and once he had given up the chase she continued on in steady flight, putting the live-oak country behind her.

She was not yet ready to turn toward home. Still impelled by loneliness and discontent, she traveled east instead. More than a hundred miles from the place she had quitted, she came to the great Okefenokee Swamp, trapped in a huge natural saucer thirty miles across, sending its dark, stained waters to the sea by way of the Suwannee River.

Like the live-oak country, the Okefenokee was a place different from any the she eagle had ever seen. Watery channels threaded it, leading from one lake to another, with now and then an island of dry land that was little more than a timbered hummock. Great rafts of water chinquapin, the bonnet of the swamp people, shaded the water, and everywhere cypress trees lifted their feathery green crowns.

This was a lush land where wild things, especially those that like watery places, lived in great abundance. Fish, alligators, snakes, raccoons, marsh rabbits, bobcats, ducks, grebes, and herons made the swamp their home. The hunting here was as easy as it had been in the live-oak country, and the eagle stayed on at the Okefenokee for weeks.

In the end she did something that was foreign to her kind and that came close to costing her life.

On a morning in February, soaring above the border of the swamp where the wilderness of water gave way to small farms, she spotted prey of an unusual kind on the ground below.

A tumbledown house of unpainted sawmill lumber lay below her, and in a log pen in the yard half a dozen young pigs were sunning themselves, watched over by the sow. They were hardly bigger than rabbits, white and tempting prey, and the eagle came about in the air.

Then she dived.

Because of the narrow confines of the pen, she did not strike at the end of her dive as she usually did. Instead, she perched on the pen's top log, waiting, singling out one pig for attack. And while she waited the sow rushed at the fence, red-eyed with rage, voicing her anger in growling grunts.

When the eagle was ready, she dropped toward her prey in a swift, wing-borne leap. But the sow was too quick for her. The froth-flecked jaws missed her lowered feet by inches and she swerved up and hung hovering a few feet overhead.

She tried three times, but the sow was a razorback, lean and gaunt, quick in her movements as a cat and, now that her young were threatened, dangerous as a bear. The small size of the pen hampered the eagle, and each time she was compelled to veer off and climb out of reach. The hog was beside herself with anger now and her grunts had mounted to ear-splitting squeals.

From the weather-beaten house there came the sudden slam of a door, and then a tall, lank man in jeans was running across the yard, holding a double-barreled shotgun ready in his hands, shouting as he came.

The eagle fled.

Luckily for her, there was a live oak close beside the pen. She put it between herself and the man and when he saw her again she was beyond the killing range of the gun, climbing swiftly. She felt shot strike her wings and body before she heard the two heavy reports, but the lead pellets were nearly spent. A few loosened feathers drifted off on the wind, but her skin was not broken and she continued to climb until from the ground she looked no bigger than a small hawk.

Behind her, the swamp man fumed and swore in futile anger. A week later he shot a brooding female eagle from a nest five miles from his place, and killed the male when it returned to the aerie, in the mistaken belief that it was one or the other of this pair that had attempted the raid on his pigpen. By that time the female that had attacked the pigs was six hundred miles from the Okefenokee, on her way home.

By hunting around the buildings of men she had broken a law that her kind rarely violated. The thundering crash of the gun's twin barrels and the stinging impact of the shot were lessons she would not forget as long as she lived.

And now the memory of that encounter merged in her avian brain with the growing impulse to go back to the Sleeping Bear country. She put the Okefenokee behind her that same afternoon, flying with steady purpose to the northwest, seeking remembered landmarks that would guide her home.

She was within a few miles of the Mississippi, in the northwestern corner of Tennessee, when she came to as strange a lake as any on this continent.

Here, a century and a half ago, an earthquake had tilted the land so that a bayou of the great river that flows only a few miles away ran backward for many days, filling and flooding a sunken basin between five and ten miles long.

Men call it Reelfoot. Much of it is shallow, and cypress trees grow out of the water—singly and in clumps—giving it a curious appearance of half lake, half swamp. The bottom is strewn with stumps and logs, left when the timber drowned and fell after the lake was formed. Those underwater tangles are rich pasture grounds for fish of many kinds.

The abundance of her favorite prey persuaded the she eagle to interrupt for a few days her homebound flight. She also loitered because she was still searching for an unmated male, wanting urgently the company of her kind. But the homing urge was growing stronger each day now. It would not be denied much longer.

On a morning at the beginning of March, perched in a dead cypress, she saw a solitary eagle coming along the shore. She screamed to attract attention, a cry of longing and invitation. Then she waited where she was. The oncoming bird answered, and from the timbre of the voice she knew it to be a male.

He swept the sky in wide circles, calling, urging her up to join him. But when she kept her perch he slanted down and alighted beside her. It meant nothing to the female that he had strange patches of white in his plumage where no white belonged.

They stood close together for a time, making low chirping sounds. At last they touched bills in a gesture of mutual understanding and acceptance. In that instant, in some fashion that men will never fathom, the bond of their kind was forged between them. They were paired eagles now.

They began the flight north the next day, courting as they went. The female led the way unerringly to the nest on Siskowet Lake where she had reared young for two seasons. They reached it the first week in March.

In no living thing do the tides of spring surge more fiercely than in the eagles. Their courtship is a ritual of wild grace and beauty, its consummation a rapturous moment of conquest and surrender. The love urge commands them totally while their season lasts, and they may couple a hundred times or more before their ardor wanes.

Khan and the she eagle made their first nuptial flight three mornings after they returned to the nest. They stood close together on the rim of the great platform for a time, chirping softly to each other. Now and then Khan opened and flapped his wings much as a crowing rooster does, and a few times his powerful yellow feet contracted into balls with a tension he himself did not understand.

The two of them left the nest together finally, soaring in wide circles above the timbered mountains. They climbed gradually in narrowing spirals, for the most part in silence, or speaking to each other in a low chittering too soft to be heard by human ears on the ground below. At intervals, however, Khan voiced his mounting ardor in wild screams. Now they drifted together, almost close enough to touch, and made sudden feinting pounces at one another. Again they separated, each performing his aerial minuet as if the other were not present.

They were dots in the vast blue vault of the March sky, and the snowy Sleeping Bears below were a faraway carpet of black and white, when the she eagle dived. She folded her wings and fell, faster and faster, reveling in the rush of air around her. This was her element and that speeding dive was a thing she had been born to do.

A hundred feet above the treetops she opened her wings and braked her fall, dropping the rest of the way to the nest in graceful sidewise dips like a falling leaf.

She perched quietly and stood watching the sky, waiting for Khan to follow her. And suddenly the distant speck began to grow and she knew he was coming to answer, falling as she had fallen.

He alighted beside her and they stood so for a long time, close together, while the desire to possess and be possessed mounted in them as it does in humans at such a time. Now and then the she eagle reached out and laid her head against Khan's neck, preening him with soft strokes. In response, he turned his head and their bills touched gently.

When their desire grew intolerable, and the time came for her surrender, she flattened her body on the nest, her head outstretched and low, and lay with half-spread wings, quivering like a fledgling bird pleading for food, in an attitude of utter enticement.

Khan was on her in a single swift movement, his body bent down like a drawn bow, seeking hers. They coupled and for a quick space of time their flesh was one and their ectasy, in that magic and mystical instant, was as great as that of human lovers. For Khan and his mate this was a seal, a tacit pledge of the bond that would hold them both in thrall henceforth. From that moment, for as long as they lived, they belonged together and to each other. All others of their kind that came near the Great Nest would be driven off as interlopers, including even their grown young when another season came for nesting and rearing. The bond was understood and unbreakable.

THE OSPREYS

The ospreys came to the Sleeping Bear country in April, on a warm and sunny day when the aspens were shaking out their silver gray catkins so that the lower slopes of the mountains and the valley of the Laughing Whitefish seemed to wear a veil of pale smoke.

Big and beautiful birds of prey, only a little smaller than Khan and his mate, the ospreys were white underneath and dark above, with long angular wings brown-barred below. They were fish eaters, liking no other food with the exception of an occasional water snake or frog, and even these they took rarely. If they turned to warm-blooded prey it would be only under the goad of starvation.

They were also the most expert fishermen among the winged predators, excelling even the eagles in skill. And because of their daily need to hunt fish they would nest nowhere except in the near vicinity of water.

This was a young pair, coming up from the southland mated, ready to build their first nest. Fifty years before, their kind had been common summer residents all along the shore of Lake Superior and on the big lakes and rivers far inland. Now they had diminished in numbers to a point where Dave Barrows had in his records only five nests in active use. Why this had happened no man was sure, for the waters where they hunted their food were as yet but little poisoned by chemical sprays, and their enemies were few.

The young pair found a nest tree that suited them exactly. At the top of the falls on the Laughing Whitefish a tall hemlock had died years before. The bleaching skeleton stood now with its top broken out, a gray stub that leaned above the river, with dry branches at the top like the spokes of a crude wheel.

Such a dead tree, ending in a broken tip capable of cradling their bulky nest and with no branches above to hinder their coming and going, was the nesting site the ospreys preferred to any other, although in times past their kind had been known to nest on chimneys, on abandoned windmill towers, on pinnacles of rock, and even on stumps and boulders and low hummocks on the ground.

The young male was first to see the stub, bare and stark against the white curtain of mist that drifted up from the waterfall. He planed down to it and the female followed.

They had come two hundred miles since daybreak, flying above land and water; much of the time they had courted. They perched now at the top of the stub and inspected it minutely. Satisfied at last, the male opened his powerful wings and soared up, and again the female was close behind him.

They began then an aerial dance much like that of Khan and his mate, soaring, circling, turning, and dodging, pursuing one another in swift and intricate patterns of flight, voicing their joy and ardor in fierce shrill screams.

They wheeled and dived across the blue vault of sky for half an hour. Then the female suddenly broke off the rapturous dance, turned, and slanted to the stub they had chosen for their nest. She alighted at the very tip of it and stood quiet there, watching her mate. He made a single wide circle far above her, set his wings, and planed down to her.

When he was only his own wingspread above her he leveled off and hung in the air, hovering and screaming, and she flattened herself in readiness for him. He dropped to her, standing on her back, keeping his balance and supporting his weight with his wings, so that the talons that could lock into and lift a five-pound fish did her no harm. His body arched down to hers, and for a brief but impassioned space of time, in the manner of all living things, the flesh of male and female became one. It was a fierce and ecstatic mating, one that would be repeated many times in the days ahead.

They began the nest building the following morning. The male gathered the material and brought it to the stub, stooping on dead tree branches as he would stoop on a trout, some of them four feet long and as thick as a man's wrist, striking and breaking them in full dive. Carrying them to the nest site, he always turned them in his feet so that they pointed in the direction of his flight, exactly as he did with captive fish.

At the stub the female took the material he brought and arranged and wove the sticks and twigs into a sturdy platform, securely braced on the branches of the hemlock. When the nest was completed it would have filled a medium-sized washtub, and it was anchored over the broken tip of the stub solidly enough to withstand wind and storm. Nests like it had been known to stand for half a century of use, until the tree that supported them crashed to the ground.

The work of building was finished in a week. The last step was to complete the nest with a soft lining of dry grass and green pine twigs. It was ready then to receive the eggs for which the two had begun it.

Beneath it, fifty feet down, the falls of the Laughing Whitefish plunged, hung with mist, into their rocky gorge. The thunder of the dropping water would be in the ears of the ospreys day and night as long as they used the nest, but this they would accept willingly.

The day the nest lining was finished the female laid the first of her three eggs. The rest of the clutch would follow, at one-day intervals. Before the last egg was laid, the male osprey had come under the watchful eyes of Khan and the eagle had launched himself on the act of piracy that for two hundred years and more has earned his kind, from the lips of many men, the contemptuous name of robber.

The osprey hunted that morning at the upper end of Siskowet Lake. A feeder stream entered there, running crystal clear over a bottom of clean gravel, and steelhead trout were entering it on their spawning migration.

A big female had excavated a shallow oval redd at the lower end of a fast riffle, clearing with powerful sweeps of her tail a space as wide as her body and half again as long, letting the current carry away the sand and debris. The bare gravel lay now ready to receive her spawn.

She was resting in the redd, her tail frayed from her exertions, her belly swollen with twin sacks of roe that held six thousand eggs. She would cast them all, and the milt of one or more males would make them viable, but of that number fewer than a dozen offspring would survive the hazards of the stream and grow to spawn in turn.

A male of her own size lay in attendance on her, only inches away, a wonderfully beautiful fish, bronze green above, silvery white below, with a rose pink stripe running down each side from gill to tail, its color heightened now with the excitement of the breeding time.

Off to one side and a few yards below three other males waited, not daring to challenge the lord of the redd for possession of the female, but loitering in the background, hopeful of an opportunity to cast milt over the spawn of the female before the drama was played out.

Cruising slowly overhead at treetop height, following the turnings of the stream and searching the water with marvelous vision, the osprey saw the cluster of fish holding motionless in the current, outlined against the clean gravel.

For a moment the bird hovered as a sparrow falcon does. Then it half folded its backswept wings and dropped.

The dive was a thing of superlative grace and speed. One of the male trout that lay downstream from the redd was nearer the surface than the rest, and it was that one the bird chose for the target of its stoop.

It struck the water breast first, with wings held high over its back, and went down to the fish like a broad-bladed arrow. Its feet were perfect tools for what they had to do: of the four toes, the outer could be turned toward the rear to team with the hind one, the two pairs locking prey like the matched jaws of an armed vise. The soles of the toes and of the feet themselves were studded thickly with short spines that fitted together like miniature armor, to keep a firm grip on the most slippery fish. And the talons that served the toes were long and curved and keen-pointed as a honed awl.

The osprey came to the surface and paused, supported on its wings, shaking the water from its plumage. The steelhead weighed a little more than three pounds, and the bird rose from the river in slow and labored flight, carrying the fish in both feet. As soon as it was clear of the water it turned the trout head on, to lessen the air resistance.

The male flew down Siskowet Lake toward the Laughing Whitefish and his nest, intending to share his catch with his mate.

Perched on his lookout tree beside the Great Nest, Khan saw the heavily burdened hawk come over the upper end of the lake, flying a hundred feet above the water. He watched, unmoving and silent until it came opposite him. His fierce yellow eyes kindled then with sudden battle lust and he launched himself with a single scream of challenge.

He overtook the osprey as a peregrine falcon overtakes a duck. It swerved and dived to evade him, then tried to climb. He swept above it and plunged, not quite striking. Again the fish hawk sought to escape but the weight of the trout it carried was too much of a burden.

The eagle rose and stooped again, checking itself once more when its talons were brushing the back feathers of the hawk. The osprey screamed shrilly in mixed anger and fear. It was fifty feet above the water now, with no chance of regaining its lost altitude, and there could be only one outcome.

On his third dive Khan struck with his feet balled like mailed fists. The blow sent the osprey reeling in the air, and it released its hold and let the steelhead fall.

The eagle twisted and flashed after it in a dive so swift and graceful that it made all the maneuvering of their combat seem clumsy by comparison. Twice the length of his own wingspread above the water, Khan overtook the falling fish and locked it in his claws.

The osprey lifted and flew on, pummeled and shaken, still screaming in fright and rage. The eagle turned in indolent flight toward his aerie.

For Khan, the taking of the trout from the osprey was no act of theft or piracy. His kind had always robbed fish hawks of their prey in that fashion. He was stronger and swifter of wing than the osprey or any other thing that flew above the Sleeping Bear country. He was the king, the proud fierce overlord of the sky above that wilderness realm. By the instinctive code that governed him and the lesser creatures around him, it was his right to take toll where and when and how he chose. He had deprived the osprey of its catch as indifferently as his father before him had deprived the young goose of her life. All that mattered was survival, and to survive he needed food. He claimed as he could.

The osprey left its own nest site an hour later and returned to the stream where the steelheads were spawning. It caught a smaller fish on a clear gravel-bottomed riffle, and flew back to its mate by a roundabout route, just clearing the treetops, hidden from the eagles by a timbered ridge.

The theft of its catch was a price it would pay many times as the summer went along, as often as Khan, if he or his nestlings chanced to be hungry at the moment, saw the osprey homeward bound with prey.

For the most part he attacked as he had that first day, climbing above the osprey and stooping on it until it surrendered its prey. Not again during the summer was it necessary for him to strike the hawk at the end of his dive. It had learned its lesson, and on his first or second pounce it gave up and dropped the fish.

A few times Khan varied his tactics, coming up under the osprey instead, seizing the fish while the hawk still held it and wresting it away with his weight and strength and superior skill in flight.

Twice after the fledgling eagles had taken flight from the Great Nest, Khan and his mate found the osprey with prey and attacked together. Those encounters were short. The hawk, sensing great danger to himself, let his catch fall the first time the eagles stooped at him, and fled without even his usual screams of protest.

Watching from his blind at the Great Nest one May morning, Dave Barrows saw Khan intercept the osprey and take from it a medium-sized fish that he took to be a sucker. Again that day, as he did so often, the eagle swerved aside and dived as the fish was dropped, overtaking and seizing it in the air, in flight so fast and perfect that it was hard for human eyes to follow.

"You may be a pirate, Khan," Barrows murmured to himself, half ruefully, "but at least you're a royal pirate." The incident did not surprise him; he knew this was a toll the eagles would exact as long as the hawks nested in their vicinity. He knew too that there were those who thought the bald eagle merely an errant thief and who found little splendid about him, who thought he did not deserve to be the symbol of America, gracing her coins and the standard of her flag. *The ways of wild things are different from ours,* thought Dave. *Theirs is a world without pity: the strong and fearless survive, the weak and fearful die. Those birds deserve to be our emblem of freedom and nobility.*

Barrows had had the Great Nest under observation for seven seasons now. At the end of the second summer he had put up a steel tower close beside and partially screened by the branches of the Norway pine. It was tall enough to command the interior of the eagle aerie and was topped with a roomy crow's nest. The blind looked out for miles in every direction over the tumbled peaks and valleys of the Sleeping Bears, and its human occupants could watch and photograph all that went on in the nest of Khan and his mate.

There was rarely a day now, from late winter until the fledglings took flight, when Barrows or one of his students did not keep watch there from first light to dusk.

Only once during the entire summer did Khan emerge defeated in an encounter with the osprey. That happened in July, when the young fish hawks were half grown and his own fledglings were almost ready to leave the nest.

Hunting along the Laughing Whitefish that day, he chanced to pass directly over the osprey nest, low above the timber, at a time when both of the parent birds were present, feeding their growing family.

The female saw him first and lifted from her bulky platform in arrow-swift flight, screaming her rage. A dozen yards behind her the male followed, uttering a series of shrill, ear-splitting whistles, feathers lifted on the top of the head to form a strange ruff between the piercing yellow eyes. The two swooped at the eagle simultaneously.

Taken by surprise, Khan tipped in the air and fended the

first attack with his great wings. But the ospreys only swerved aside and pounced again, and that time the male struck him a hard blow on the back, so that feathers drifted on the wind. An instant later the female flashed so close above his head that her talons brushed him.

When they stooped the third time, the eagle turned on his back in the air and lifted his mailed feet to meet them, in the immemorial battle pose of his kind, as he would have met harassing crows or herons or other birds. But against the pair of fish hawks the ploy served him poorly. The male, diving on him, dodged aside and the female came in from one side and clubbed him on a wing with the full force of her plunge.

The battle was fought in the nest territory of the ospreys and he was the interloper. The territorial rights of many birds, especially the big raptors, are fiercely defended, and the intruder who infringes on them senses instinctively that he does not belong there. For that reason he is more easily driven off.

At his own aerie, the eagle would have fought one or both of the ospreys to the death. Here he lacked the stomach for such combat. When they came in a fourth time, more reckless than ever, he sensed himself the loser.

He dived away from them, wheeled, gained altitude swiftly and left them to their own affairs. Not again that season would he venture close to the hemlock stub that held their nest.

THE GYRFALCON

Khan and his mate reared two fledglings that summer and saw them out of the nest in late July. Three months later the bigger of the two, the young female, was lost to the poacher Nunn.

She was hunting along the Lake Superior beach a dozen miles from the Great Nest the day he killed her. Nunn was hiking that day along Mirror Creek, a small stream that came down from the western slopes of the Sleeping Bears, scouting for beaver sign, laying plans for the outlaw trapline that he would set out before freeze-up.

The young eagle sailed over his head, turning in indolent circles, paying no attention to the man moving stealthily through the undergrowth below her. Nunn stopped and waited patiently, and after a few wide turns she planed down and settled in the top of a tall lightning-killed cedar.

The trapper made his stalk with craft and caution, moving

in the cover of young evergreens as cautiously as if his quarry had been a deer. He slammed his shot at fifty yards and the eagle was knocked from the tree as if by a giant hammer. Nunn collected her wings and tail plumage and left the carcass where it fell.

In December, when the eagles were ready to quit the Sleeping Bear country, he killed the second of the year's young, the male, and so wiped out the increase that Khan and his mate had accomplished for the year. Over the country Nunn ranged, the odds were mounting against any gain in the eagle population.

The week that Khan and his mate started their leisurely drift southward, over the timbered country and farmlands that lay beyond their home mountains, Nunn walked into Baldy Vachon's unpainted store at Pine Stump, nodded Baldy toward a back room, and dumped the contents of a gunny sack on a counter there. The sack contained the coveted plumage of a dozen eagles, about half in dark juvenile color, the rest revealing by the pure white of the tail plumes that they had come from adult birds.

"There's another pair I could take like falling off a log," the poacher told Vachon. "They got a big nest in the mountains, on Siskowet Lake. But some damned professor has put up a tower there, and you never know when he's going to come snooping around."

"Better leave 'em alone," Baldy advised. "You need a few pairs for seed anyway, or you'll run out of birds."

Three hundred miles to the south of the Great Nest, where a deep-currented river flowed into Lake Michigan, Khan and his mate found an unexpected treasure-house of food.

The winter was early that year and a flight of goldeneye and old-squaw ducks had moved south ahead of their usual schedule. Finding open water and a teeming supply of small fish in the deep pool of the river just inland from the sand dunes of the beach, they had lingered there. They would stay as long as the food lasted and the pools remained open, which this season would be throughout the winter.

As often as the current carried them to the lower end of the pool, they rose in short swift flight and returned to its head, then drifted down again, diving, playing in the water, gabbling and talking among themselves. In all the dune country there was no merrier sight.

There were about fifty old-squaws in the flock, migrants from a far-off land, a lighthearted and frolicsome band like no other waterfowl of the northern hemisphere. They had come down from nesting grounds on the bleak Arctic barrens along the rim of the continent and the islands beyond, to the east and north of Hudson Bay. Their summer home they shared with snow geese and swans, and also with Arctic foxes and polar bears and the fierce snowy owls of the barrens.

They were the noisiest of all ducks, and it was their flock talk and ringing call notes that set them apart from others and also that accounted for the curious names bestowed on them by hunters in the places where they wintered, on the Great Lakes and along the coast of the North Atlantic: such names as Injun duck, ow-owly, oldwife, and sou-southerly. The notes were loud and clear and far more musical than those of most ducks. On the upper Yukon in the early days, the fur traders had even given them the name of organ ducks because of their harmonious voices.

There was in the makeup of Khan some peculiar trait, not common in his kind, that impelled him to the red flesh of birds as readily as to the fish that are the preferred diet of the bald eagle. When he found the flock of winter ducks loafing at the river mouth, he plunged instantly to attack.

Both the goldeneyes and old-squaws were as deft in the water as the eagle was in the air, and the life-and-death contest was a strange one. Nevertheless, the outcome was not genuinely in doubt from the first instant.

The bird Khan chose for killing was an old-squaw drake, a small, singularly handsome waterfowl, white and brown and black, with pearl gray flanks and a pert pointed tail almost as long as his body.

The flock fell silent as the eagle dived at them, scattering and diving in panic, old-squaws and goldeneyes alike. Since the threat came from the sky, none of them tried to take flight. Instead, one after another they flashed beneath the surface of the pool.

The splashing subsided and for half a minute the place seemed deserted save for the eagle, hovering just above the water on swiftly beating wings.

The drake Khan had chosen went deep and streaked across the pool. Among all the waterfowl of North America, none outranked him at diving. He was capable of staying submerged for a full minute, and more than once his kind had been caught in gill nets set 180 feet down in the water. Only the loon excelled him as a diver.

But this time his skill and endurance would avail him little. As he fled beneath the water, the eagle stayed directly above him, following him without difficulty in the clear dark depths. When the old-squaw's air supply was exhausted and he bobbed to the top, the eagle was waiting no more than a wing length overhead.

The duck gulped air and dived again, but his stay underwater was not so long this time. Again he rose to the surface, and again the great raptor waited at the exact spot. This was a form of hunting every eagle understands, and for Khan the kill was no more than a question of time.

Around the pool other ducks were surfacing for a brief instant, refilling their lungs and diving to safety once more. But they were not pursued as the old-squaw drake was, and they could take the time they needed. To none of them did the eagle give the slightest attention. His eyes, afire with the lust to kill, stayed riveted on the drake, and at the end of each dive he crowded it more and more mercilessly.

When the drake surfaced for the fourth or fifth time it was too tired for another escape dive. It floated with head and back exposed for a single second, and the eagle dropped and locked his talons in its flesh. The kill was an instant thing, and he lifted with it and he and his mate flew together to a sheltered spot at the top of a low dune. There they fed.

The capture of an old-squaw or goldeneye became for Khan a daily ritual after that. The female eagle stayed with him for a week, killing twice on her own, but she lacked his appetite for the flesh of other birds, as well as his savage patience and skill, and in the end she left him and flew south. Khan stayed on.

The winter days grew colder, and the river pool was skimmed with ice around its edges. Snow fell, turning the tawny dune country immaculately white, and the ice built into a shelf along the shore where the ducks rested and preened. But there was still open water in the center of the pool, where the current moved through and food was abundant, so they lingered.

The hunting was easy and sure, and there was no reason for Khan to leave. He went each morning or evening to the river to take a single bird from the flock. When spring came he would return to the Great Nest, and instinct told him the female eagle would join him there if she survived the winter.

Toward the end of his stay, a rival hunter found the ducks and he had a competitor.

The newcomer was a white gyrfalcon, wandering south from the same bleak and lonely land where the old-squaws summered. It had its nest on a sheltered ledge, high on the face of a cliff that looked out over a gray arm of the sea where pans of ice floated and ground together, and there the falcon and his mate had reared their fierce fledglings for seven seasons.

The falcon was a hunter of birds, scorning ground prey save on rare occasions. A colony of small auks had nested for generations at the foot of the same sea cliff that housed the hawks, hiding their eggs in crannies among huge boulders on the beach. There were thousands of the pretty black-and-white quail-sized auks in the colony, and it was from them that the pair of falcons took most of their food. There was a heap of auk bones on the ledge beneath the hawk aerie, mute testimony to the tribute they exacted.

The other winged prey on which the falcons relied were the ptarmigan that nested on the treeless barrens inland from the sea. Both auks and ptarmigan were taken in the same way, pursued and killed on the wing. Now and then, when the auks were absent on their winter migration and the ptarmigan were in short supply, the gyrfalcons killed lemming or the white Arctic hares, coming to the ground to clutch as the lesser hawks did. But that was not a way of hunting they liked.

It was a die-off of ptarmigan that had sent the lone white falcon roving south. The auks were wintering along the stormy New England coast, two thousand miles from their summer home, and when the supply of land birds began to fail the hawk was compelled to migrate.

He discovered the band of ducks in the pool at the river mouth on a crisp cold morning, and perched in a convenient tree to bide his time. He did not have long to wait.

In midmorning a pair of goldeneyes lifted from the water and swung out over the broken ice fields of Lake Michigan in an exercise flight. The falcon watched them go, and gave chase as soon as they were away from the timber behind the dunes.

The pursuit was of short duration. The ducks saw the dreaded predator coming, high above them, and, terror stricken, they separated and fled across the ice fields. But the chase was like that of a greyhound following a hare. The hawk flew at twice the speed of his prey, and when they broke apart he chose the drake and was over it, a hundred yards up, in seconds. There, without pausing, he stooped.

There are few sights in the world of wild things more terrible and yet more thrilling to watch than the almost vertical dive of a falcon on its prey. Man will never be able to measure the flight speed of that chilling attack, but it has been estimated as high as two hundred miles an hour, and the best observers think that is not exaggerated.

When he was directly above the fleeing drake the falcon tipped down, driving himself with a few swift wing strokes until he was falling almost too fast for the eye to follow. Then he half folded his long pointed wings and became a streaking white meteor. Had a man been near enough he would have heard a noise like ripping canvas as the hawk cleaved the air.

He did not check himself. At the last instant he tilted so that he struck the duck feet foremost, his talons closed into mailed fists. The blow struck the drake on the back where neck and body joined, and it died almost without feeling the impact of those fists. A small cloud of feathers drifted off with the wind and the goldeneye plummeted to the ice, lifeless and limp.

A single shrill scream of triumph broke from the hawk. He swept on until the momentum of the stoop was spent, banked, and dropped after his victim in wide, looping flight. He stood beside it for a brief space of time, inspecting it with mixed hunger and fierce joy in the kill. Then he clutched it and lifted, carrying the two-pound drake with effortless ease. On a low dune top half a mile away he perched and began to pluck away the breast feathers and feed on the warm red flesh.

Thereafter, for the remainder of the winter, Khan and the gyrfalcon shared a common hunting ground. In the near vicinity of their nests neither would have tolerated the other. They would have fought, and for all its speed and fearlessness the hawk would almost surely have died. Here in an open land of lake and river and dune and forest, they avoided each other and no enmity developed between them.

Khan returned to the Great Nest on a morning in early March, when a heavy fall of wet snow was swirling across the Sleeping Bears like thick white smoke. He planed down to his lookout tree and perched there, watching the nest through the curtain of the storm. In the center of the wide platform lay an alien object, something that formed a low mound covered with snow. At one end of the mound two small horns stood erect, like short stubs of branches on a rounded block of wood.

Staring at the nest, Khan suddenly knew that snow-covered lump for what it was. In his absence, a pair of great horned owls had taken over the platform. The female was there now, brooding on her own eggs.

What he could not know was that the owl had laid her clutch of two at the end of February, after the early-nesting fashion of her kind. They were within days of hatching now, and the fierce, implacable mother would not surrender the nest willingly.

But she had no choice.

The eagle flew instantly to the attack. The owl saw him coming but did not give ground. Khan landed on the edge of the platform and for a brief space of time the two faced each other.

The owl rose to her feet, with spread wings that spanned half the length of the eagle's, uncovering the pair of round white eggs that lay warmed and protected beneath her. Her round yellow eyes glared at the eagle, blazing with hate. She hissed to warn him off, and the mandibles of her bill snapped together time after time with a sound as sharp as trap jaws closing.

But she was outweighed and outmatched and she knew it. When Khan pounced at her she rose in swift, soundless flight. He followed her into the air, and she struck at him savagely. But he met the attack in routine eagle fashion, rolling on his back and lifting his terrible feet to meet her. She dodged aside, and when the same thing happened three times she fled with the eagle close behind. He would have caught and killed her but for the fact that she dived headlong into the treetops where he was not willing to follow, threading her silent way through the branches with marvelous skill.

She tried twice to come back and reclaim her eggs, but each time he drove her off and in the end she gave up.

Khan's mate came back two weeks later. They flew together to the nest and perched for a time on its rim, talking to one another in low chirping tones. Now and then the female stroked Khan's neck briefly with her bill.

Finally they lifted in nuptial flight, came back to the big platform and coupled twice in swift succession. Later, they began the spring task of repairing and enlarging the nest. When they finished, the two eggs of the owl lay, stained and forgotten, under a thick layer of twigs, dry grass, and long gray strands of Usnea moss.

Their eviction from the big nest they had appropriated had strange consequences for the owls. In a hollow stub at the top of a half-dead birch a mile away they found a new nesting site. They mated again, and night after night their deep hooting and wild catlike screams of courtship, sounds as blood-chilling as human ears will ever hear, rang through the dark woods.

When she was ready the female laid two fresh eggs and began once more the task of incubating. The time then was mid-April. For one reason or another, perhaps because she had remained away from the nest too long on a hunting trip and they had been chilled, these eggs were infertile. This, by the instinctive processes that governed her behavior, she was slow to realize.

It was not until early July, when she had brooded on them for the better part of a hundred days and they were rain-stained and blackened, that she understood at last that her long patient vigil was fruitless.

The stub where she had nested was open at the top, where a big branch of the birch had broken away many years before. Its hollow went down five or six feet, floored at the bottom with wood chips and dry debris. The owl had made no real nest, content to bed her eggs on that material. Running up the stub, at the level of her eyes as she brooded, was a crack some two inches wide. She had used it as a peephole while she stayed on the eggs, enabling her to keep watch over the woods around her. Now she put that crevice to an almost unbelievable use, arriving at a reasoned decision and carrying out deliberately an action of a kind that man does not often credit wild things with being capable of.

With her breast, she pushed the two discolored eggs out through the crevice one at a time, so that they fell and shattered on the ground below. Next she signified to the male owl that she was ready to breed again, and when July was coming to an end she laid once more, a single egg this time.

It hatched in late August, and when the hardwood foliage around the stub turned red and gold at the beginning of autumn the single owlet was still a fledgling in the nest, feathered and more than half grown but not yet ready for flight.

Of that long summer, the female had spent a total of almost five months brooding on her three separate sets of eggs. In all the literature of birds there is nothing recorded to match her amazing record of patience and constancy.

THE GOLDEN KIN

A thousand miles distant from the Great Nest, down the westering track of the winter sun, another aerie lay bedded on a rim-rock ledge overlooking a wide sweep of sun-parched hills, dry stream courses, and sagebrush flats.

It had been there, in the Rio Blanco country on the western slope of the Colorado Rockies, almost from the time the Great Nest was begun in the tall pine in the Sleeping Bears. But it was a far different structure, built of dead sagebrush, sticks, and weed stems, hollowed at the center like a shallow saucer, with a lining of rabbit fur, soft grass and lichens, and a few green leaves. Low and bulky, it was wide enough for a tall man to lie outstretched across, but in height it would have reached no farther than to his belt.

It belonged to a pair of golden eagles, proud and fierce

raptors that were akin to the white-headed clan to which Khan and his mate belonged, yet differing from them in many ways.

The golden eagles were part of a population of their kind found around the northern half of the world. Their kind nested in the north of Europe and in Asia as well as in North America, and in winter were even seen in Africa. Not so the bald eagle. As far back as it has been known to man, it has been a bird of this continent alone.

There was no white in the plumage of the golden birds. Their backs and breasts were rich dark brown, and the only ornamentation was the golden hackles that rose on their heads and necks and gave them their name. In youth, before the white head and tail were in evidence, it would have been easy to mistake a descendant of Khan for the other species, but, for those who knew birds, one telltale feature told them apart. The golden is a booted eagle, with feathers down his legs to the toes. The lower half of the shanks of the bald eagle are bare, covered with hard scales. Those naked tarsi, featherless from knee to foot, are the hallmark of all the sea eagles wherever they are found.

Apart from these differences and the kind of country they preferred, perhaps the greatest difference between the two eagles lay in their choice of food. The whiteheads were basically eaters of fish, most of them turning to other prey only when their favorite food was hard to get. The goldens, by contrast, wanted red flesh, mammals or birds, and of the two they seemed to have a preference for furred prey, perhaps because it was easier to take. They disdained fish.

One fundamental thing the two had in common. They killed to live, but they were also born to kill, taking a fierce delight in their hunting. No man, seeing the aerie on the Rio Blanco crag and the other in the Sleeping Bears, separated by a third of the width of the continent, would have had the slightest reason to think that the two proud males that owned and defended them would one day fight to the death.

On the March morning when Khan drove the usurping owl

from his nest the two golden eagles were moving north from their wintering area along the Rio Grande, flying above the desert that lay beside the Pecos River.

They were hungry and hunting as they flew. A strong headwind buffeted them, but they rode it easily, the tips of their great wing quills spread like the fingers of a man's hands, wind slots that let them keep their balance and stability with little effort. A Scottish gamekeeper, watching them and knowing well the ways of their kind, had once commented that in a gale that makes it hard for a man to stand these eagles are as steady as the rocks below them.

The male was moving a thousand feet above the desert when he saw movement below him and close to half a mile ahead.

The snake was a western diamondback, five feet long, as thick of body as a man's forearm. It lay against a rock, enjoying the warmth of the pale March sun but half shaded by a low clump of winter-dead grass.

Everything in the desert was dust colored now, the first sparse green of greasewood and other dry-country shrubbery not yet showing, and the rattler was dust colored like the rest. Its heavy coils matched so perfectly the sand and rock and dead grass around it that a man, especially one not accustomed to the ways of the desert and its inhabitants, might have walked within striking range of that deadly coil, might even have stepped on it, before he suspected it was there.

Only one part of the snake's body would have betrayed it. The last foot of the stubby tail was marked with strikingly contrasting rings of black and white. They accounted for the name of coontail by which desert men commonly knew it. But the tail was resting now under the coils of the body and the whole reptile was no more than a small dusty hummock under the clump of dusty grass. In all the desert it would have been hard to find a more perfect example of natural camouflage.

Had the snake stayed motionless, even the wonderful eyes

of the eagle, eyes that could discover a jackrabbit a full mile off, probably would have passed it by. But the sun crept around the rock, uncomfortably warm, and the snake moved, shifting its position to stay in the broken shade of the grass. The eagle detected that slight movement on the motionless background of earth and sloped down in a long unhurried dive.

Two paces from the rattler, just beyond reach of its strike, he alighted and folded his great wings, the fierce brown eyes flaming with hunting lust.

The snake saw its danger. Its thick neck and the forward third of its body lifted and arched into a menacing letter S, ready to deal the blow of death. The tail was also lifted, the sprung rattles set up their dry continuous whir, and the black forked tongue flicked in and out from the flat triangular head.

How did the eagle understand the danger that lay in those sullen coils? Was it no more than instinct? Or had his kind learned, over a thousand generations, that the strike of this snake meant death? However he came by the knowledge, he possessed it and it ruled him now.

He was not afraid of the diamondback, for fear was not a part of his makeup. He was of the clan that falconers had trained to fly at wolves on the steppes of Siberia, the great and splendid birds that once in Europe none but kings could fly. But the absence of fear did not make him reckless or careless.

He danced away, then hopped suddenly almost within reach.

The snake did not take the bait. It remained looped and ready, the buzz of the rattles went on without interruption, the black tongue continued to dart in and out.

Half a dozen times the bird feinted, coming closer and closer, and suddenly the neck and half the snake's body straightened like a whiplash, driving the fangs for their target.

The eagle was too quick. He leaped back and the strike found no mark.

The bird baited his prey into three such strikes, each a blur of movement too fast for the eye to follow, each ending in empty air. On the fourth attempt the diamondback was a fraction of a second slower in recovering his fighting pose, and the eagle leaped and pounced and caught him outstretched.

The talons of one foot locked in the flat head, the other foot found a grip at the midpoint of the snake's body. It was over in seconds. The long, powerful creature twisted and sought to coil, the tail lashed in a brief death frenzy. Then the rattler relaxed its entire length and the eagle rose and flew off with half his quarry dangling beneath him.

On a flat boulder a mile away he perched, tore off the head and gulped it down. In the craw of a bird or in the stomach of a man the deadly venom of the snake would be as harmless as water. It must be injected into the flesh and reach the bloodstream to wreak its terrible havoc.

The she eagle flew to the rock and joined her mate and the two of them fed together. The snake weighed almost half as much as either of them, and it was an hour before they left the boulder and winged north again in unhurried flight.

Three days later they were at the home aerie and the work of overhaul was begun, broken time after time when they soared into the limitless sky in courtship and came back to the ledge to couple.

The female laid her two eggs three days apart, and the second was no more than in the nest, warm and secure under the soft plumage of her breast, when the blizzard struck.

It was a savage storm, with a white smother of snow, and roaring winds and bitter cold. It lasted for twenty-four hours, and when it ended the Rio Blanco country lay under a white blanket that covered the ground to the depth of a man's knees and was in places drifted five times that deep.

In that white world of intense cold the wild things huddled, fasting, moving only if they had to. For the eagles hunting was futile.

They had gone a day without food while the storm lasted.

For two days afterward the male quested in vain, while his mate stayed on the nest, warming her two eggs. Then he found prey of a kind that only hunger would have driven him to attack.

The buck was a mule deer, two years old. The previous autumn he had carried a rack of antlers with twin points on either side. Western hunters would have rated him a two-pointer. As such things are reckoned in the East, he would have been called a four-point deer.

He had dropped the antlers at the usual time, in December. They lay now at the bottom of a timbered draw, buried under the snow, and his new rack had not begun to grow, so that his head was as bare of ornament as that of a doe.

In the fall, fat and sleek, he would have weighed 135 pounds, but winter browse had been scarce and he was 25 pounds lighter now. Nevertheless, his weight was still almost tenfold that of the eagle.

He came along a well-traveled deer runway, walking slowly in belly-deep snow. When the eagle saw him he was in an open place, without shelter. Ordinarily he would not have quit the cover of timber by day in this fashion, but he was on migration and the urge to keep moving drove him.

The mule deer herd to which this young buck belonged numbered in the thousands, and their spring and autumn trek was the last of its kind left on the western slope of the mountains.

The herd wintered in an area of dry hills on a north-flowing branch of the White River. In spring they began a march eastward to high country around Trappers Lake, at the headwaters of the White, moving singly as the young buck was doing, by twos and threes or in bands of a dozen or more. The Trappers Lake country was their home for the summer. In October, when the first heavy snow fell there, the return migration down the White got under way.

This was no short seasonal movement of the kind mule deer and elk make in many places in the West, coming down a few miles from high country in autumn to winter range in sheltered valleys at lower altitude. This was a true migration. The summer and winter ranges of this herd lay fifty miles apart.

There were many such migrations of mule deer in the old days, in many states. Roads and increased hunting ended them. There was even one of whitetails in the Lake Superior country where Khan and his mate nested, north in spring to the open timber along the shore of the big lake, back in autumn to the shelter of evergreen swamps a hundred miles to the south.

The deer moved in such numbers there that Indians built converging fences of brush and small trees to funnel the migrants to the shore of a lake and force them to swim across. The Indian hunters camped on the far shore and killed a winter's supply of venison from their canoes, while the deer were helpless in the water.

It was the building of railroads that brought that migration to an end, many years ago.

But the mule deer of the Rio Blanco country continued to make their long seasonal marches, and so it was that the golden eagle, whose aerie was only a mile away, surprised the young buck, helpless in the deep snow.

The eagle stooped on the deer as he would have stooped on a jackrabbit, falling almost vertically, at a speed as great as that of a stooping peregrine. The buck had no warning. The bird struck him on the back of the head with both feet, a blow that drove him to his knees in the snow, and before he could stagger up, the curved steel claws of the hunter were buried in his neck in a grip that a man could not have broken with two hands.

The buck reared on its hind legs, flailing the air with its forefeet, but totally unable to reach its tormentor and too stunned by that first blow to make its efforts count.

It backed into a tall clump of mountain mahogany, weaving and twisting, and went to its knees again. And while it fought for its life the eagle was fighting savagely, pitilessly, to kill. Killing meant food, and food meant survival for the great golden raptor and his mate.

The neck of the deer was torn open now and the snow

where they fought was trampled and stained with blood. The buck struggled to its feet a second time, and then the eagle drove talons into the spine and the battle was over. The deer fell and did not get up. The bird lifted and took a single short turn in the air, screaming to his mate. Then he settled to the snow, tore open the soft underbelly of his kill, and began to fill himself from the steaming entrails. The female heard his far-off cries and came to him in swift straight flight. When they left the deer they were as gorged as a pair of vultures. No matter the weather now, the carcass of the buck would keep them safe from hunger while the brooding of the two eggs continued in the nest on the ledge.

But in the interval while the she eagle fed with her mate, misfortune had befallen. One of the eggs, the second laid, chanced to lie half exposed on the aerie lining, and before she returned and settled on it, the cold March wind had chilled it and killed the embryo within.

The remaining eaglet hatched in April, a helpless, down-covered chick that gave little promise of the swift and powerful raptor it would be, as is true of all fledgling birds.

Its first meals came from a jackrabbit that the male hunted and killed and carried to the nest, its weight taxing his powers of flight to lift it. The female tore off tiny bits of the red flesh and fed them to the fledgling bill to bill. But as the weeks passed and he gained strength, he began to tear at his own food, whatever it was.

The list was long. Jackrabbits, cottontails, prairie dogs, now and then a small marmot, sage hens and sharp-tailed grouse, an occasional bull snake, twice domestic turkeys from a farm ten miles distant, and, four times before the fledgling left the nest, a small lamb taken from the grazing flock of a sheep herder in a nearby valley.

It was that raiding of domestic sheep when the opportunity offered, although it happened only a few times in a year, that had won the eagles the undying hatred of all sheepmen and that in the end would have disastrous consequences for this pair of goldens.

On a sunny morning in June, when the young eaglet was half grown, the adult male, riding the wind several hundred feet above the sage-covered flats and searching the ground below with the fabulous eyes that were tenfold as keen as a human's, saw a strange sight.

On a low, rocky hummock, grown up with sparse grass, two snakes were upreared, facing each other, half their bodies raised vertically off the ground.

They were prairie rattlesnakes, close to four feet long, heavy of body but not as thick in relation to their length as the diamondback the eagle had killed in March.

They stood only a foot apart, the tail of one thrown across the body of the other as if to serve as a brace, and they were weaving back and forth in an incredible, sinuous dance.

A human seeing them—and hardly more than a handful had ever witnessed this reptilian minuet—would have said that the snakes were courting. Given a second guess, he probably would have surmised that they were dueling to the death. But he would have been wrong both times.

While the eagle soared above them, dropping lower for his attack, one wrapped itself about the neck of the other and threw its opponent forcibly to the ground. The fallen snake reared itself again, standing as tall as its weight could be supported, and the strange slow swaying went on.

They did not rattle or attempt to strike. The time was June, weeks after the mating time of their kind was past. Oddest of all, perhaps, both snakes were males.

The purpose of that undulating dance? No man knows. It has been reported among snakes of many kinds in many parts of the world, as well as among half a dozen species of rattlers on this continent. For want of a better explanation, men who study the ways of reptiles call it a combat dance, but it is hardly true combat, for neither of the participants undertakes to injure the other.

Can it be simply a reptilian display of sexual urge, stimulating the two participants long after the passing of the season when a female of their kind will accept them? Who can say?

The hunting eagle had no interest in the oddity of the ritual or the causes that inspired it. He saw the two rattlers only as food, and his circles narrowed until he was directly above them, a hundred feet up. He dropped then like a meteor, braking his fall at the last instant and touching down lightly just beyond striking range of the snakes.

They separated and one looped in battle coil, buzzing a warning. The other undertook to slither off among the rocks, and the eagle struck it from behind in a swift pounce. His talons closed, one foot in the reptile's head, the other in its body, and without waiting for it to die he lifted and flew toward the nest. There he tore off and swallowed the head, and left the body to the young eaglet.

TO THE DEATH

The fledgling left the nest in free flight a month after the male brought the rattlesnake in for food.

By sheer coincidence, that same day Hal Staveley parked his four-wheel-drive truck at the foot of a long ridge, in a spot where it was hidden by a thick growth of pine and juniper, and began a slow and careful climb to the crest.

Staveley was a predator control officer, in the employ of the federal government, charged with the task of keeping in check the populations of such wild hunters as coyotes and mountain lions, and with doing away with individual animals—bears and eagles included—that raided livestock or poultry farms.

He had worked at the job for more than twenty years, using the tools of his trade, including hunting hounds, traps, and poison. As time went on he had come to dislike the methods that meant indiscriminate killing of any and all predators in the territory he covered. Some creatures, getting a taste of mutton or beef or, in the case of the mountain lion, even of the flesh of young colts, turned persistently to such a diet and had to be eliminated. But Staveley greatly preferred hunting down these lone killers whenever he could, leaving untouched the great unoffending majority of their kind.

For that reason, he had turned to the use of a predator call to lure in, within gun range, the animal he needed to destroy. It was highly selective, and if he was hunting a pair of sheep-raiding coyotes and a mountain lion came stealthily to him instead, in response to the agonized rabbit squeals of his call, he would stand up, wave his hat at it, and let it go.

This particular day it was a lone coyote that he hoped to lure in. A sheep rancher had lost a dozen ewes and lambs in a single recent night, and careful study of the slaughter had told Staveley the probable identity of the killer. It was his duty to rid the valley of that coyote, and calling was his choice of method.

The wind was blowing over the crest of the ridge, which was the way he needed it. He left his truck very quietly, careful to slam no doors or make commotion of any kind, and his climb was cautious in the extreme. If the coyote was bedded on the sagebrush flat beyond, as he had cause to believe, and if he gave it the slightest inkling of his presence his errand would be a waste of time.

Soundlessly he made his way up the hill. At the crest he did not walk across; instead, he went to his hands and knees so that he would not be silhouetted against the sky. He crept over and moved to a clump of serviceberry a dozen feet down the opposite slope.

He sat in front of it, needing the thicket behind him to break his human outline but also needing an unobstructed view in front and to right and left. He was wearing camouflage clothing and there was scant chance that an approaching preda-tor would make him out. Resting across his lap was the double-barreled shotgun he would use for what he had come to do.

He waited briefly, taking into account the fact that despite his caution his quarry might have heard some slight sound of his approach. If it had not sighted him and if he gave it a few minutes to forget whatever had alerted it, no harm would be done.

Finally he lifted the predator call to his lips and sounded the anguished, squealing screams of an injured jackrabbit. He put into the series of cries all the agony and terror he could, trying to mimic the sounds of a rabbit caught and dying a tortured death, knowing that the more pain and fright he voiced the more sure his quarry would be to respond. After a minute or so he let the cries die slowly away. Then he gave a sudden loud scream, as if the dying rabbit were suffering all over again. The calling was briefer that time and as it trailed away in pitiable whimpering he saw not the coyote he hoped for but a fox coming headlong up the slope.

It was a young animal, three-quarters grown, and it was running recklessly to make a kill of its own on the wounded rabbit. Staveley made no sound or movement as it charged up the slope, and when it stopped it was only a dozen feet from him, eyes blazing, ears laid flat.

Puzzled now as to the exact whereabouts of the prey it had heard, it stood still for a minute, then began to walk slowly back and forth, every muscle of its body alert and tense, listening, peering this way and that into the brush.

Staveley watched it with mixed amusement and annoyance. He would have preferred not to have this interruption, and yet, as always with an animal tricked by calling, he was fascinated by its behavior. There was nothing between him and the fox save a small log on the ground, nothing at all to hide him, and a dozen times it stared straight at him. Yet it had no inkling that a man was near.

After two or three minutes it sat down in front of him like a small red dog. He was sure that if he used the mechanical mouse squeaker cupped in the palm of one hand he could bring it closer, perhaps close enough to touch. He had once had a coyote come up behind him as silent as a falling leaf, not knowing he was there, his first warning when he felt hot breath on the back of his neck. He twisted around and the animal was crouched less than a yard away, teeth bared in a vicious snarl.

Almost certainly he could bring the fox that near if he chose. But he knew that if it took sudden alarm and fled, and if the coyote he was hunting happened to be approaching, the running fox would frighten it off. So he sat motionless and waited.

Neither the fox nor the man had warning. A broad shadow swept across the open ground between them, Staveley heard the rush of great wings through the air, and the eagle struck like a thunderbolt. It was the golden male, stooping on the fox from behind the ridge.

The bird struck and clutched, but the fox twisted in its grip, biting and scratching, and broke free. They fought a ground battle then, with Staveley an astonished spectator. They feinted, leaped, slashed with talons and teeth, the eagle buffeting with his wings, the fox using the thick soft brush of his tail to shield his head and neck.

He darted suddenly under the wings, locked his teeth in the muscles of the bird's breast and hung on. The eagle tumbled backward, then, unable to free itself, tried to lift clear of the ground. For two or three times its own length it dragged its strange burden. Then the laboring wings gained a purchase in the air and the bird rose in heavy flight, with the fox dangling by his own teeth, too enraged to release his hold. They were a dozen feet up, twenty, then fifty, and Staveley realized that the animal had waited too long.

At a hundred feet his jaw muscles tired or he lost courage. His teeth slipped free and he fell, turning over and over in the air. He struck the rock-strewn ground with a dull thud, writhed briefly, and was dead. The eagle, freed of its burden, climbed slowly and went out of sight beyond the ridge, flying toward its distant nest, hampered by the burning pain where the vulpine teeth had gone deep. It made no effort to come back and claim its kill.

That was the first time in his life that Hal Staveley had seen an eagle bested in fair fight, and he found the whole strange encounter hard to believe. No longer interested in his own hunt, he put away the predator call and went back to his parked truck.

Almost two months after Staveley had watched that amazing battle, tragedy of an odd sort overtook the male eaglet the pair of goldens had reared during the summer.

Matching his parents in size now, a skilled and relentless hunter in his own right, he was patrolling a big sagebrush flat a dozen miles from the aerie where he had grown to adulthood. The sage lay sere and silvery in the October sun, with a dry watercourse winding across the flat, but on the foothills beyond, the aspen groves made patches of vivid yellow, and along a distant river cottonwoods were a golden ribbon, unfailing signals that autumn was at hand.

The young eagle was hungry. He had hunted through the morning without sighting quarry. Once he had wasted an hour circling above a prairie-dog town, but the increasing chill of the nights had sent the inhabitants of the town down to their underground nests of dry grass, and his patient airborne vigil was of no avail.

When he sighted food at last it was not prey. It was a dead jackrabbit, dangling from a low branch of a juniper tree, half a man's height from the ground.

The young golden had no aversion to descending to the role of scavenger on occasion, and now his hunger made him even more willing than usual. He tipped toward the distant bait and went down to it in a slanting dive. As he touched the ground beneath it he heard a sharp metallic snapping sound and a spring-loaded snare of steel wire closed like trap jaws around one leg.

The leg broke under the blow of the tightly drawn wire, and agony stabbed through the thigh muscles of the great bird.

He leaped frantically into the air, but the tendons of the broken leg held him and the length of snare jerked him back to the ground again.

Though he fought blindly all through the afternoon, there was no escape from the merciless grip. At nightfall he lay with outstretched wings, exhausted, half dead from thirst. The cool of the night revived him and when day broke he resumed his struggles, leaping, twisting, falling back, resting only when he was too worn for further effort.

He lived through the heat of the day and through another night. In midmorning of the third day, as the October sun climbed higher and the heat turned oppressive, death finally released him from his agony.

It had been a cruel and shameful death for such a bird. The snare had not been set for eagles. The trapper who placed it and covered the open loop of wire with dry grass and duff, and then hung the jackrabbit over it for bait, hoped to take a bobcat or coyote. But it was a method of trapping that was becoming increasingly common in the golden eagle country now, and more often than not it was an eagle that fell victim.

Before the year was out, a federal game management agent would make an investigation of the eagle kill in seven counties of a western state. His shocking conclusion was that in a single year trappers using such snares had caught not fewer than twenty-five hundred eagles. Of that number between six and seven hundred were known to have died in snares tended only once in ten days, or been killed deliberately by the trapper. How many more had been released only to die later of broken legs and other injuries, no man could guess.

In November the two adult eagles left the Rio Blanco country for the winter. Moving south, they came to a broad slope of mountain where sheepherders pastured flocks numbering in the thousands. The owners of those flocks, claiming that eagles were making serious inroads when the lambs were young, had launched an illegal and merciless war against the big raptors.

Golden and bald eagles alike were the targets, and helicopters and small fixed-wing aircraft the instruments of destruction. The stockmen behind it, men of wealth and political influence, were untroubled by the fact that the laws of the country gave total protection to all eagles. With open contempt for the law, they hired the aircraft and the men who flew them and did the gunning, confident that the law would not be invoked.

Before the year was out the law would be invoked, and some shocking revelations would result. A helicopter pilot would testify under oath that he had helped in the killing of six hundred eagles and been paid fifteen thousand dollars for the job, and a rancher who flew his own aircraft would be proven guilty of shooting three hundred more.

There were men who understood well enough that unless such slaughter could be stopped the eagles were doomed as a race. Unluckily, they were not men in positions of control, and when the eagle-killing cases came to court money and influence outweighed the lives of the great birds and little was done.

The golden male and his mate were drifting across a wide valley, five or six hundred feet above the ground, on the morning the hunters found them. The light plane came over the valley at twice the altitude of the two birds, enabling the pilot and the gunner with him to look down from a higher elevation than that at which eagles normally cruised. This made it easy to spot any target within sight.

Fear of aircraft was a lesson the eagles had never learned, unless it became plain that they were actually being pursued. Pilots carrying out big-game research, such as a census of antelope herds, had learned long before that they must remain alert to the presence of goldens and avoid the birds to escape collision. Many times such pilots had been compelled to break off their game counting because of an eagle that refused to move out of their flight path.

So it was only natural that the golden male and his mate should pay little attention to the Super Cub as it came droning above them. But then the pilot saw them and slanted down in his gunning approach, and when he came near they separated and fled.

The hunters chose the female because she was nearer. The pilot wanted to make a level fly-by just to one side of her. He aimed his plane accordingly, and the chase began.

The eagle was capable of flight speeds of at least two miles a minute, but only for short distances, under the press of fright or in pursuit of prey. In any lengthy chase she would tire and the aircraft would have no difficulty closing on her. Even the small helicopters commonly used in mountain country, able to maintain level flight speeds of eighty or ninety miles an hour, were fast enough to outrun an eagle.

As the Cub came near, the female did her best to evade it and escape. She twisted, rolled, turned, and dived, much as she would have done in combat with another of her own kind. But the aircraft was tireless and relentless. It followed her every turn, pressing her down toward the ground. When she sought to gain altitude, it outflew her and drove her even lower.

In the end she was trapped against the vertical face of a butte, with no room to maneuver. She fled along it; the hunters overhauled her swiftly and made their fly-by only fifty feet away. The gunner lifted his automatic shotgun and fired twice.

One of the magnum charges of No. 2 shot caught her squarely. The great she eagle crumpled. Her shattered body fell in a slow pinwheel spin and struck at the base of the rock wall.

The male eagle had gone to ground, hiding under an overhang of rock. He stayed there until the plane gave up the search for him and left the valley.

Two weeks later disaster befell that same pair of hunters, as they harried a young golden above the sagebrush in a valley twenty miles away.

They crowded close, and when they made their fly-by the bird swerved and dived. The pilot tipped the plane on one wing and turned in a vertical bank, and in that instant the gunner, seeing a chance of a hit, fired three shots. One of them cut away a strut of the aircraft. A wing failed and the Cub plunged down. Rescuers found the two charred bodies in the wreckage.

The story went out, and other hunters, already concerned about the risks of low-level flying over rough and broken terrain, with treacherous wind currents off the ridges, began to back away.

At the same time, the law was amended in Washington to provide sterner penalties, including revocation of the license of any pilot found guilty of taking part in eagle-hunting. The outlaw war on the big birds suddenly lost appeal, to a point that the chief of law enforcement of the United States Bureau of Sport Fisheries and Wildlife could say, "We hope the shooting of eagles from aircraft is now past history. A job already unpopular with most pilots because of its difficulties and dangers has at last been made untenable."

The male golden from the nest on the Rio Blanco ledge never knew whether it was the loss of his mate and his fledgling, or some vagary in his own brain, that impelled him to break off his flight southward the day the female was killed, turn east instead and fly for many days above flat plains and woodlands that were totally alien to him and his kind.

He wintered in eastern mountains, on the upper waters of a great river that goes down across New England to the sea. Rabbits and grouse and waterfowl were plentiful enough and he did not lack for food. But there was no other eagle of his own kind within two hundred miles of him, and it was a winter of discontent. Before it ended he wandered on, turning southward now, so that early March found him at the head of Chesapeake Bay, where the spring flight of ducks and geese was leaving for northern breeding grounds. The hunting was good, and he followed the great waterfowl migration across the northern states and into Canada. Then, with the winter at an end, the urge to go home and find a mate overwhelmed him, and he set his wings against the warm southwest wind and began the journey of two thousand miles to the crag in the Rio Blanco country.

Square in his path, although he could not know it, lay the

Sleeping Bears and the aerie in the tall pine where the two whiteheads kept vigil.

The encounter occurred on a morning in April.

Watching from his lookout perch, Khan saw the strange eagle coming long before human eyes could have made out a speck in the distant sky. He watched while the interloper grew steadily larger. At two miles his keen eyes could make out every detail of the other bird—the dark plumage, the booted legs, the wingspread that matched his own. This was not an eagle of his own kind, and he waited no longer. He launched himself with fierce screams and flew to give battle.

The golden male saw him coming and knew him for what he was, a foe and challenger, but did not deign to turn aside. For these two fierce and majestic lords of the sky there could be no retreat and no quarter. One must die, and they were evenly matched.

Each weighed a little more than twelve pounds, and for their weight they were the strongest things that flew. Each had a wingspread a foot longer than the height of a tall man, and the skill of one in diving and turning and rolling in the air was as great as that of the other. Each had feet that could all but cover an outspread human hand, and the muscles that controlled the curved daggers of the talons were capable of driving them entirely through a duck or rabbit or marmot at a single thrust. And once locked in flesh, those talons were close to impossible to loosen.

Either of the great birds was capable of striking the life from the other with one blow. Once the claws found their mark, death would be swift in coming. The only thing that mattered was which could strike first.

They came together feinting and barrel-rolling, climbing, each striving to rise above his adversary, to gain sufficient height for a lightning-fast stoop, but they were too closely matched for that.

They mounted higher and higher in the air with wild

screams, pouncing, striking, wheeling away, fending the blows with their wings, protecting breast and belly and head, probing for openings like aerial swordsmen. Blood was drawn on both sides and feathers drifted down. Birds less powerful and savage would have tired and broken off the battle, but for them that could not be.

They were so far aloft in the vast blue bowl of the spring sky that from the ground they looked no bigger than the smallest hawk, when the golden male, rolling away from a swift thrust of the whitehead's talons, misjudged by the length of one of his own wing plumes. For a fraction of a second his underbody was exposed.

Khan rolled belly up, as a leaf turns in the wind, and reached with his great feet. The claws went home in belly and breast, and the golden male began to die.

He still fought back with beak and talons, clawing like a great winged cat, but he could not find the vital spot he wanted, and second by second the strength went out of him. The two fell slowly, locked together in a final embrace of hatred and rage, wings flapping to slow the fall. At the end the golden male was hanging limp in the grip of his enemy.

They touched the ground with Khan above, standing on the other's body. The dying eagle quivered briefly and was still. After a minute the whitehead loosened his hold, hopped away, and rested briefly before he rose to fly back to the lookout tree beside the Great Nest.

THE SLOW POISONS

Khan's kind was diminishing in numbers now, not only in the Lake Superior country but all across the eastern half of the continent.

Coming up from the south five springs before, migrating later than was his wont, he had seen on the ground below him men driving machines across fields and up and down long rows of trees, with a white fog drifting from the machines, spreading on the wind like smoke.

He could not know it, but that fog was made up of chemical poisons. The spray rigs were signing a death warrant for the eagles that hunted and nested in the region where they were used. Execution of the warrant would be slow, but it was as certain as the changing of the seasons.

The poison sprays were long-lasting. They were meant to kill only insect pests, nuisance birds and animals, and weeds and brush, but it was inevitable that they should be washed into ditches and streams and carried finally to the waters of the big lakes and even to the sea. There would begin a curious process of buildup along the food chain that locks all living things in an inescapable web.

Few people understood it, for it worked in strange ways. Men of science talked of the poisons in terms of parts per million, offering the comparison that one part per million could be thought of as one ounce in a thirty-ton carload of flour, or one short step in the total walking distance between New York City and Niagara Falls.

The bottom mud along a shore where the land was heavily sprayed with the poisons might contain no more than a hundredth of a part per million, an amount so infinitesimal that it did not seem possible it could pose a threat to any living thing.

But the creatures that lived in that mud and in the water above it, and in the air over it and on the adjoining land as well, possessed the strange ability to take in the poisons a little at a time and store and accumulate them in their bodies until they sometimes reached concentrations a hundred thousand times as great as that in the bottom mud.

The buildup began with the aquatic insects and tiny crustaceans on which the smallest fish fed. It was not uncommon for them to contain fifty times the amount of the poisonous residues found in the mud around them.

The fish that preyed on them continued the process of accumulation, carrying in their bodies three or four parts per million of the deadly compounds. The larger fish that were next in the food chain also stored the poisons, and built them up as high as twenty parts per million.

At the top of this water-dwelling chain stood the fish-eating birds, the loons and grebes, gulls and terns, ospreys and eagles.

Gulls that preyed on the contaminated fish accumulated the poisons until their fat held more than two thousand parts per million. They began to lay eggs with shells so thin that the brooding females trampled and broke them. And of the chicks that hatched many died from the high concentration of poison in their frail bodies, passed on to them through the eggs. Ospreys and eagles were faring no better.

Even birds that did not eat fish were not safe. The peregrine falcon, a magnificent raptor that preyed solely on smaller birds, began to disappear outright from its former haunts. Bird men were puzzled as to the cause, but studies in England, where the falcons were also declining at a shocking rate, solved the riddle. The bodies of those found dead contained heavy amounts of chemical poison of one kind or another, and it was clear that the residues were reaching them through their food chain. The small birds they killed and ate were contaminated by their own diet of insects. They passed the poisons on to the hawks, and the concentrations finally became greater than the peregrines could tolerate.

If any one of the poisons had been taken in greater dosage and all at one time, it would have brought death certainly and promptly. In fact, the amount required to kill a mosquito or an eagle, or even man himself, was roughly the same on a weight-for-weight basis.

But because they were ingested very slowly, a minute quantity at a time, the victim had a chance to store them in an unchanged state in the fat of its body, where they were relatively harmless. Not until they reached a high level of accumulation, a process that might take years, would they exact their ultimate toll. But in the meantime, passed into the eggs of fish and birds, they doomed the offspring.

No more than a handful of farsighted and thoughtful humans were aware of the extent of this poisoning and concerned about its consequences. It had reached a point now where there was no water, fresh or salt, anywhere on the face of the planet that was not tainted. Even the remote Antarctic continent, thousands of miles away from the nearest land where any spraying was done, had not escaped. Seals and penguins in that far-off place now carried traces of the poisons that had reached them, as they reached all living things, through food chains.

The source of it all was not hard to discover. Use of the poisons had become incredibly widespread.

In the southern United States five million acres of land were sprayed with two of the deadliest known compounds in a war intended to eradicate the fire ant. The cost was fifteen million dollars, the result worse than failure.

Far from being wiped out, the ants had invaded an additional eleven million acres while the campaign of extermination against them was going on. But the wild birds and animals of the region did not escape so easily.

Raccoons and quail all but disappeared. Wild turkeys plummeted in numbers. Countless woodcock, feeding on contaminated earthworms, died.

In the West someone made the discovery that a chemical marketed for fly control would kill off unwanted birds if it were sprayed or painted on surfaces where they alighted. It was used near cattle feedlots, and thousands of doves were killed.

Also in the West, millions of acres of land were sprayed to kill sagebrush and allow grass to come in for grazing. Sage grouse died out with the brush.

In eastern Canada, in one five-year period, five million acres of forest were sprayed to control an infestation of budworm. The poisons found their way into the waters that supplied fish hatcheries. Most of the young salmon in the hatcheries were lost, wild fish populations slumped, and fish food was eliminated in the rivers involved.

Lake shores in New England were sprayed to rid towns, resorts, fishing camps, and cottages of mosquitoes and blackflies. Salmon populations dropped to the vanishing point.

Spraying for thistle control caused a heavy kill of trout in one state, and the use of poison to kill vegetation in drainage ditches had the same result.

In the lower Mississippi, between Memphis and the Gulf of

Mexico, five million to ten million fish died in one winter from the use of a single poison.

Use of the compounds even on a small scale had the same deadly results.

Villages sprayed with certain chemicals to kill elm beetles, in the hope of checking the spread of Dutch elm disease, and wiped out their robin populations along with the beetles. A rancher sprayed his cattle and washed the equipment in a nearby creek. The side result was a kill of all fish and fish food in miles of stream. A sheep dipper let poison wash into a creek and eighteen thousand fish died. A Midwest farmer cleaned his potato-spraying rig at a bridge over a trout stream, and killed every trout for miles below. In a western state a lake was sprayed to eliminate a nuisance population of gnats. Although the poison used was in a concentration of only two hundredths of a part per million, a colony of grebes that stood at the top of the lake's food chain of plankton and fish concentrated the compound up to two thousand parts per million. In one year the grebes had suffered a severe die-off and had ceased to breed.

So it went. Few human beings were aware of the magnitude of the spraying program or the size of the industry that made and sold the poisons. More than sixty thousand formulas for different compounds had come into being, the eight hundred million pounds that were being manufactured each year were worth more than a billion dollars, and the output was doubling every ten years.

For the fish-eating eagles and ospreys there could be only one result. Wherever the sprays were used their kind was doomed, and the end was coming in sight.

Every scientist who was studying the birds of prey was aware of the slow decline and its inexorable threat, and without exception they were deeply concerned about its implications. But they were powerless to effect a remedy.

The records of Dave Barrows told a sorry story.

Twenty years earlier, he had known of fifty pairs of eagles

that nested and reared young around the Great Lakes and on their big islands. The count now was down to ten active nests. Then the year came when of those ten only Khan and his mate and one other pair produced fledglings that lived to leave the aeries in free flight. When that happened, Barrows knew that the end for his beloved and splendid raptors was not many years away.

Ospreys were vanishing at an even faster rate. He had reports now of only three nesting pairs in all the area of forest and water where he kept records, and if those three reared a single fledgling in a season he considered them fortunate.

Next there came a spring when the she eagle at the Great Nest left off her brooding in mid-April. When she and Khan did not begin the usual feeding of young birds Barrows realized that something was amiss. He climbed to the aerie. The thin and broken shells of two eggs lay on the trampled grass lining.

PLUME HUNTING

There was a lesser reason, but one with more immediate consequences, for the dwindling numbers of eagles along the southern shore of Lake Superior. The feather trade was taking a steady and relentless toll of the birds that remained.

It was a two-man operation. Bill Nunn, the poacher and outlaw beaver trapper, did the killing, without pity or regard for the consequences. Baldy Vachon, at his ramshackle store at Pine Stump, bought the feathers from Nunn and disposed of them. It would have been hard to find a more unsavory team or one better suited to the illegal business.

In his early years Baldy had operated a prosperous speakeasy in the Saint Clair Flats area at the head of the Detroit River. But he had the misfortune to incur the displeasure of a big-time rum-runner who was bringing Prohibition-banned liquor across from Canada, and word came to him, via an unsmiling messenger, that he was scheduled to go for a swim with cement blocks wired to his feet.

Very sensibly, he cleared out and lay low in another state until the threat appeared to have blown over. When he judged it safe to surface, he went to the Lake Superior country and bought the rundown general store at Pine Stump. It was a comedown, but hopefully it was a way to stay alive. Adding the Starlight Bar to his holdings was an idea he thought up later, when Prohibition was out of the way.

Two buildings, both unpainted and weathered, made up the business district of Pine Stump, in cutover country a dozen miles inland from Lake Superior. They were the store and the saloon. Ten or a dozen small and squalid houses straggled away from them along the dirt road that led south across the Yellow Dog Plains (once pine-covered, but logged and barren now) to the paved highway.

Baldy managed the store by himself. He hired a thick-necked ex-lumberjack bartender to take charge of the Starlight.

The saloon's incongruous name was hand-lettered in red paint on a plank above the door. Inside, a battered bar that had seen more elegant days in a saloon and brothel in a bigger town during the logging days ran half the length of the place along one side. Booths along the opposite wall, three or four tables with rickety chairs, and a jukebox completed the furnishings.

But for all its poor appearance, the money that went into the cash register on Saturday nights, and on some other nights as well, would have made happy the proprietor of many a better establishment.

As for the store, it was a slovenly place, showing no evidence of prosperity. But it paid off, in various ways. A stranger walking in to make a small purchase would not have guessed that through the back room, a lean-to built on at the rear, more than five thousand dollars worth of contraband beaver pelts passed in an average year. And through that same room flowed a steady trickle of eagle plumes supplied by Nunn, small in volume but sufficiently large to constitute an unbearable drain on the eagle population left in the region.

Plume hunting was nothing new. Close to a hundred years before, in the swamps of the South, a feather trade of incomparably greater scope had flourished, a cruel and bloody business that was all but forgotten now.

It was aimed at two white members of the heron tribe, the lesser and the greater egret, and before thoughtful and concerned men finally succeeded in outlawing it and enforcing the law it had brought both birds to the very doorway of extinction.

It was based on the feminine fashions of the time, coupled with the fact that as their breeding season neared these tall and graceful birds put forth magnificent nuptial plumage in the form of long flowing plumes, known as aigrettes, growing on the back between the wings and extending far beyond the tail like a bridal train.

Both sexes wore these splendid lacy plumes. Some birds bore as many as fifty, graceful and flowing, as immaculately white as newly fallen snow. They appeared in January and February, in time for the elaborate courtship ritual of the egrets, and before the young birds were out of the nests in June or July they were shed.

In the latter half of the last century these ethereal feathers were prized by the millinery trade above all other ornaments, and the egret slaughter reached a magnitude that is hard to believe.

It began in Audubon's time, around 1840. He told of a plume hunter who was offered a double-barreled shotgun in exchange for a hundred long whites, as the egrets came to be known in the trade, and who delivered that number freshly killed the following day. By 1900 the egrets had reached their nadir, and among the pioneer conservationists of that day there was little hope they could be saved. As they became scarcer the price of plumes soared, until it reached thirty-two dollars per ounce, about twice the worth of their weight in gold, on the London market.

One writer told of 1,608 packages being sold at London auctions in a single year, each package weighing about thirty ounces. The plume hunter calculated that an average of four birds were needed to supply an ounce of plumes, which meant a total of almost two hundred thousand killed to supply a single auction house.

At the turn of the century a prominent bird protectionist warned that no rookery of the egrets could long survive unless guarded day and night by force of arms.

Like all the herons, the birds tended to be solitary in their habits save for one period of their lives, the times when they nested, and when they hatched and reared their young. On their hunting grounds, stalking frogs, small fish, and snakes in marshes and along the shores of ponds and shallow lakes, they were most often seen singly or in small numbers.

But when the time came to nest, they congregated in crowded colonies, sometimes numbering hundreds or even thousands of birds, often in company with other members of the heron family, perching their frail nests in the tops of trees or brush.

This habit of colony nesting left them hopelessly vulnerable to the plume hunters, and although they were shy and difficult to approach at other seasons of the year, once they had young in the nests they lost their normal fear of man.

If a rookery was shot up before the eggs hatched the surviving birds were likely to abandon the place outright. But as soon as the fledglings were out of the shells and the summer task of feeding them had begun, the adult egrets would return to the colony time after time even in the face of gunfire.

The plume hunters traded on this lack of wariness. They waited until a rookery was, in their parlance, "ripe," that is, until the last of the eggs were hatched, before they began their murderous work. Then they went into the nesting swamps and shot as long as their plumed targets lasted.

Early-day conservationists who visited the raided colonies

told of seeing the carcasses of scores of dead egrets strewn on the ground under the nests, each bird stripped of a patch of skin that bore the prized aigrettes.

The stench of the decaying bodies was overpowering, and in the nests above the young birds grew weaker from hunger day after day until they perished on the frail platforms or tumbled to the ground to die among the slaughtered adults.

Those who saw firsthand the results of the hunting spoke with deep bitterness of vultures feeding on the dead, of the empty nests, the sickening odors, and the silence of death that lay over the ravaged swamps. One observer even told of seeing crippled birds staked out in the marsh around a rookery to decoy others of their kind within gun range. "I have seen the terrible red ants actually eating out the eyes of wounded decoys that had been tied and propped up by the plume hunters," he wrote. "The plume trade is a barbarous thing, and the raided rookeries are a sight to make the blood boil."

Egret plume hunting ended in the early years of this century, largely as a result of unflagging efforts on the part of the National Association of Audubon Societies, and the tall and stately white herons began a slow recovery that in time would bring them back to their former abundance over most of the country where they nested.

Compared with the slaughter of the egrets, the plume trade that Bill Nunn and Baldy Vachon were engaged in was trifling and insignificant. But because it drew on a vanishing and remnant population of birds, its threat to that remnant was very real. If it ran its course unchecked, it would be the final straw in the destruction of the few eagles remaining in the region where it flourished, birds that were already drifting toward extinction.

It was done with sufficient furtiveness that few people were aware of it, and almost none understood its scope and the threat it posed.

Wildlife authorities in Washington, watching with mounting concern the nation's shrinking eagle population, were fully alert to the role played by a few outlaw feather hunters, but for the most part were helpless to stop the hunting.

Almost without exception, the illegal hunting was done by white hunters who sold the skins or feathers to Indian traders. For many years most Indian ceremonial garb had been made with substitutes for the traditional eagle feathers of the early days. Dyed turkey feathers were the chief source, but even chicken feathers had been used. There was still a strong demand for the eagle plumes that primitive Indians used, however, and with a pair of eagle wings bringing fifty dollars and a single choice feather up to twelve dollars on the plume black market, that demand was sure to be met. There have always been and always will be men like Nunn and Vachon willing to break any law for profits of that kind.

For the most part the feathers were used in regalia at Indian powwows. More than two hundred of these events were being staged annually, in every section of the United States, creating a market far in excess of anything the feather trade could supply. Indian culture enthusiasts among whites, eager to revive the tribal customs in their entirety, openly encouraged such use. Even some tribes that had not used eagle feathers in their tribal rituals originally were wearing them at the powwows now, as a drawing card for tourists. And among a few Indian groups the feathers were a required part of ancient religious rites.

Wildlife agents pressed a steady war against the plume hunting, in the face of heavy odds. Tips were infrequent and leads hard to follow. In one case the agents made seizures of fifty pairs of wings, more than the total number of eagles that still nested around the shores of all the Great Lakes, but the sentence for the outlaw hunter was a jail term of only six months. Federal judges showed little understanding of what was at stake, and little concern for the eagles that remained. Court calendars were crowded with criminal cases regarded as far more important, and it was difficult to bring a feather hunter or trader to trial. Some cases were delayed for years.

The illegal activities of Nunn and Vachon had been well known to federal and state wildlife authorities for a long time, and both men had been closely watched, for their eagle dealing as well as for other poaching and trafficking, but so far they had left behind no trail that would take them before a court.

Their time was running out now, however. United States wildlife authorities, spurred by a handful of worried conservationists as well as by their own knowledge of the feather trade, were closing in. They would resort to the one method most likely to gather the evidence they needed, the work of an experienced undercover agent, and they had the right man to do the job.

THE HUNTER

Before daybreak on a cool autumn morning in Khan's twentieth year, eighty law-enforcement officers assembled at prearranged rendezvous points in two of the leading duck-hunting centers of the nation. Some were federal marshalls or wildlife agents, the rest, state game-protection officers.

They gathered in river towns along the upper Mississippi, in Wisconsin and Iowa and Minnesota, and in Illinois along the Illinois River downstream from Peoria.

It was a big aggregation of lawmen, and it needed to be. They had a big job to do, and it must be done with dispatch and without hitches. The eighty men carried warrants for the arrest of an even hundred violators of the laws that protected migratory waterfowl. Some would be charged with market hunting, some with illegal trafficking in contraband birds.

The government had waged a long war, ever since market hunting was outlawed in 1918, against unscrupulous men who continued to kill ducks and geese for profit and against wildlife bootleggers who sold them. This was to be the biggest single roundup in the history of that war. The men who had planned it and laid the groundwork had high hopes that they were smashing at one stroke the whole market-hunting operation in the top waterfowl country of the Midwest.

The trap was smoothly sprung. Because of the size of the job and the fact that some of the wanted men had hard reputations, the officers had staged a quiet rehearsal the day before, locating the homes of the violators and sizing things up. They began knocking on doors at daybreak, and they found a majority of their men in bed, sleep-fogged, too surprised to resist or even to protest. In three hours most of the wanted hundred were in jail. Rounding up the others would be only a matter of time.

The federal wildlife authorities had dealt a body blow to a ring of market hunters that had been slaughtering and selling not fewer than a quarter of a million ducks each year.

It had been no simple operation. With few exceptions, the men who shoot for market and deal in bootleg game, whether ducks or deer, are the Bill Nunns of the world. They are petty racketeers, crafty and hard to catch, often with connections and markets reaching into the underworld of big cities where the contraband is finally disposed of. And often they are dangerous as well.

They operate in a chain. At the bottom are the hunters who do the shooting. Next come the dealers who buy the birds or deer and make deliveries. At the top are the operators of bars or restaurants where illegal game dinners are served at a fat profit.

Such rings have effective spy and lookout systems, and they are likely to have helpful connections with corrupt political figures as well. It is common for local wildlife officers to know that ducks are being shot regularly for market, for example, and even to know who is doing the killing. But it can be next to impossible for those same officers, known to everyone in their home area, to gather the evidence necessary for a conviction in court.

The early-morning roundup that brought a hundred men to account grew out of two years of skillful and hazardous work on the part of a single individual. Tony DeMarco was an ace wildlife undercover man for the United States government.

His appearance suited him for the role. Short and rotund, with heavy brows hooding the dark eyes of a born gambler, and most of the time wearing a day-old stubble of black beard, he looked what he professed to be, a shady character out to turn a fast buck, a petty racketeer dealing outside the law but not involved in anything big enough to scare off the clients he dealt with.

He had posed at times as a gambler, a dealer in hot jewelry, a procurer of call girls. But these were never more than sideline activities. Always he had the first requirement of an undercover agent, a cover, a fictitious name and place of residence and a legitimate business of some kind that he pretended to be carrying on as his main source of income. Every item of identification he carried bore the false name and address, and in each case he learned enough about his pseudo business to qualify him for a place in it.

This time he was a manufacturer's agent for a hardware maker in Minneapolis.

The president of that company was known to certain federal people as a duck hunter and dedicated conservationist. Under the name of Alarico Matera, DeMarco went to him and laid his cards on the table, explaining frankly what he hoped to do. "I want to travel as a representative for you," he finished.

The hardware man hated market hunting and all it stood for, and the thing was easily arranged. DeMarco's credentials were adequately checked, he spent two weeks at the factory familiarizing himself with the line, and hit the road. He had the cover he needed. The rest would be up to him.

He began by calling on hardware merchants in the duck-hunting towns. He carried a catalog and order blanks, and now and then he wrote a small order. But he contrived a shifty manner that kept his sales record from reaching awkward size.

Once he had laid a foundation that satisfied him, he began to look for market hunters. As he expected, his first transactions were of the penny-ante variety but they opened the door. It would take time to gain the confidence of the violators he was after.

His first buy was from a gas-station operator in an Illinois town, a man known to waterfowl officials as a major dealer in contraband ducks.

"Understand you're a duck hunter," Matera mumbled while his gas was being pumped.

"I do a little huntin'."

"I like it, but I'm a hell of a poor shot," the customer confided. "I sure wish I could find somebody that would take me out and help me kill a few."

The market hunter came to the point without hesitation. "You want to buy some ducks?" he asked.

"You bet I do!"

"Drop back here in the morning. I'll try to have a few rounded up for you."

Before noon the next day, the undercover agent traded a ten-dollar bill for five plump mallards and went his way content. The ice was broken.

Within a month he was making small buys of ducks and geese with no difficulty, in the leading waterfowl centers for a hundred miles up and down the river. The market hunters checked with the hardware dealers, and when Matera's connections were found to be genuine, confidence in him grew. Long before the duck flight moved south he was buying birds in lots up to a hundred.

By that time he had had to invent a fresh reason for his dealing. He had begun by explaining that he liked to give ducks away to his customers, that it brought him business. But now he let the word leak out that he had a friend in Chicago who served duck dinners at his bar and restaurant, and who looked to Matera as a major source of supply.

"I can handle all the birds I can get," the agent confided to a few of his top sources.

The word spread, and by the time the spring flight had passed through that area the next year he had bought more than two thousand birds. In open season he had hunted with many of the violators with whom he dealt, but always he had been scrupulously careful not to break the law himself.

There was danger in what he was doing. In a tavern one night a hard-bitten riverman who had just delivered him a lot of fifty ducks leaned across the table and said coldly, "You know somethin'? If you ever turned out to be a fed and you testified against me in court, I'd kill you on the witness stand."

Privately DeMarco stored the threat away for future reference. But he also met it head on. He shoved his face close, his eyes blazing.

"Don't you call me no lousy fed!" he growled. "From now on you can keep your damn ducks. And if you say that again I'll meet you out in the alley and cram your teeth down your throat."

"Take it easy, take it easy," the hunter mumbled. "I only said if you was."

But deep down the agent knew he was dealing with a man who would have to be watched.

When the fall flight was due the following autumn, he renewed his operation, moving into other states. Buys of a hundred birds became common now. From time to time he was offered bigger lots than he wanted, and refused on the ground that he lacked the cash to handle them. In a town on the Mississippi he made contact with a hunter who had a dozen gunny sacks of down, collected in a season and a half of shooting and stored for sale. And in a bar a few nights later, a retired policeman offered to guarantee him ten thousand ducks before the end of the season. The agent backed away, offering the excuse that that was more than he could get rid of.

One of the most curious practices he uncovered was a trick

the market hunters resorted to by way of convincing their customers that their ducks were wild, not domestic birds from a game farm. If they trapped or netted birds, as some did, they put half a dozen in a sack, backed off and fired a charge of shot into the lot to prove how they had been killed.

By the end of the second spring the agent's purchases totaled more than five thousand birds. He had turned them over as he bought them, meeting at night with federal agents in alleys, on lonely country roads, even in cemeteries. The ducks lay now in cold storage plants, each tagged as to the time and place of purchase and the name of the violator who had supplied them. The trap was ready for springing.

When the roundup was finished and court action was pending, DeMarco dryly told a fellow agent, "Well, that potlicker that threatened to kill me on the witness stand will get his chance now."

Now, a year after the waterfowl roundup, DeMarco had been given a lesser assignment and one that looked to both him and his superiors as far easier and less hazardous. He was being sent into the Lake Superior country to put an end to Bill Nunn's eagle killing.

Nunn lived with a slatternly wife in a two-room tarpaper-covered shack a dozen miles from Pine Stump. Abandoned cars parked in the yard and a mound of beer cans and rubbish at the door bespoke the character of both the home and its occupants.

DeMarco drove up to the place shortly before dark on a crisp evening in early October, knocked at the door, and introduced himself.

"My name is Toll," he said when Nunn answered his knock. "Ike Toll. I'm up here looking for some real estate for an outfit in Detroit."

"You're barkin' up the wrong tree," Nunn grunted. "Ain't no real estate around here that anybody would want, not so far as I know."

"That's not why I drove out," Toll told him. "I hear the geese are in on the Sturgeon River Plains, and the bartender at

Pine Stump said maybe I could get you to take me out in the
morning."

"Fifteen dollars for a half day," Nunn said shortly.

"That's a little steep," the agent complained, "but if I get a
couple of geese it's worth it."

The hunt was legitimate enough. Toll went through his
usual act of missing his shots. Nunn killed four geese.

"Two of 'em are yours," he said when he was paid off. "If
you want the other two you can have 'em for ten bucks extra."

It was the old familiar routine. Toll paid and took the four
geese.

He came back four or five times as the autumn went along,
hunting with the poacher, paying high prices with a little
grumbling, winning his confidence, involving him in one shady
deal after another. By the time freeze-up drove the ducks and
geese south, he had bought twenty geese, a handful of ducks,
twelve illegal beaver pelts on the pretext that he wanted a coat
for his wife, and two deer.

The last night he was in the area, he and Nunn were drink-
ing in the Starlight Bar when Toll brought up the subject that
was his real objective.

"You got any eagles up here?" he asked.

Nunn's shifty eyes narrowed and his lips drew back over his
yellowed teeth. "Now and then a pair," he conceded.

"I wish to hell I could get my hands on a few feathers," the
agent said. "Friend of mine out in Tucson is an Indian trader,
and he has a tough time gettin' them. I'm going out there for
the winter in a couple of weeks, and I'd be in solid if I took him
a bundle. They bring a good price, too."

"How much?" Nunn asked guardedly.

"I could pay forty dollars for a pair of wings, and good tail
quills are worth ten dollars apiece."

It was double what Nunn was getting from Vachon and he
was tempted, but he was not ready to drop his guard.

"I don't have any," he said. "But if you're back up here in
the spring drop around. I might be able to pick up a few."

Toll left the Pine Stump area the next day and dropped out of sight. But after he was gone, Vachon dropped Nunn a warning.

"I don't like that damn real estate guy you've been taking out," he said. "I'd say he's a phony. He reminds me of a fed I knew on the Flats years ago. I wouldn't make any more deals with him if I was you, not until we find out more about him."

"If he turns out to be a phony and he comes snoopin' around again he'll have some bad luck," Nunn growled.

"OK," Baldy agreed, "but be careful how you do it."

Although he didn't suspect it, Bill Nunn killed his last eagle the following April. They were getting harder and harder to find, and he had finally decided to risk shooting one or both of the birds at the Great Nest.

Khan and his mate had returned in March, and by the first of April the usual two eggs lay on the lining of the aerie. Nunn hiked in to the place on a morning of wind and cold rain, and watched it from a safe distance for more than an hour to make sure there was no one in or around the tower. When he concluded the coast was safely clear, he closed in and climbed to the blind.

The two eagles took flight at his approach, circling and screaming. But they were well used to man now, and once he was out of their sight he did not have long to wait. The female came back to her eggs within a quarter hour.

Nunn had no intention of killing her in the nest, since he lacked the stomach to make the climb up the trunk of the aerie pine. But when she settled on the rim of the nest and stood there briefly, surveying the timber around her, she gave him exactly the opportunity he wanted.

He was carrying a double-barreled shotgun, and the blast of shot knocked her sidewise, so that she fell to the ground like a dead leaf coming down.

Khan had circled close to his lookout perch by that time, but at the thudding report of the gun he veered off and climbed swiftly and silently.

Nunn did not wait for him. He climbed down, retrieved his kill, carried the eagle to a thicket back in the mountains, salvaged her wings and tail, and left. The feathers were worth over a hundred dollars and he counted it a good morning's work.

A week later Ike Toll showed up at Pine Stump once more. He looked Nunn up and invited him to the Starlight for a drink. At the end of an hour in the bar the poacher came to the point. "You still want eagle feathers?" he asked.

"You bet. And the price is up, too. My man out in Arizona told me when I left he'd pay fifty dollars for a pair of good wings. I don't want any commission. This is just a deal to help a friend. You can have the whole fifty bucks."

"You know where the old dump is?"

"At the end of the road west of town?"

Nunn nodded. "Bears got to workin' it, and it was closed a few years ago. Nobody ever drives in there anymore. It's a good place to meet. I don't want you snoopin' around my place if I'm gonna sell you eagle feathers. But you be there at midnight tomorrow night and I'll have somethin' for you."

Wariness stirred in Toll. He knew the place of rendezvous well. It was unvisited, as Nunn had said, and lonely, at the end of a dirt track that straggled off into the brush, grown up with grass and brakes, a perfect spot for an ambush. But the agent had kept too many similar appointments with hard characters, in the same kind of places, to back away from his opportunity. He rated Nunn somewhat less dangerous than a number of the men he had tricked and outwitted in past operations.

He drove to the abandoned dump at the appointed time and sat in his car waiting. Nunn's battered pickup truck rolled in noiselessly fifteen minutes later, lights out, and parked beside him.

The poacher climbed down with a gunny sack and handed it to Toll without preliminaries.

"There's four pairs of wings there and fifty tail feathers, all white," he said shortly. "Count 'em if you want to."

Toll shook his head. "I'll take your word, Bill. You wouldn't cheat a friend."

"You got enough money with you?"

"There's more in the sack than I expected. I lack about a hundred bucks. Can I give it to you in the Starlight tomorrow night?"

Nunn nodded, and the agent counted out a roll of bills. When he finished, the poacher turned back to his truck, whipped a worn .30–30 off the seat and wheeled, leveling it at Toll's chest.

The agent's surprise was genuine. He had hardly expected gunplay.

"Hey, what the hell goes on?" he demanded angrily. "What's eatin' you?"

"You ain't gonna be in the Starlight tomorrow night," Nunn told him. "You're gonna be down in thirty feet of water, at the bottom of the old limestone quarry south of town. You overlooked somethin', you goddam fed. Baldy still has a few connections in the right places in Detroit. They checked you out durin' the winter. You never bought an acre of real estate in your life. You're what Vachon and I thought you was all along, a lousy stool pigeon."

Tony DeMarco was in as tight a spot as he had ever been in, and he knew it. Bill Nunn was at that moment as dangerous as a coiled rattlesnake. But DeMarco knew another thing. There was only one way to meet a threat of this kind. Outbluff it.

He moved unhurriedly, dropping a hand to the barrel of the rifle almost casually, half expecting to feel the smashing blow of the shot. When it did not come, he pushed the muzzle aside, wrested the gun from Nunn, and sent it sailing off into the brush. Only then did his fingers close around the butt of his own sidearm, snugged in its shoulder holster.

"Get into my car, Bill," he ordered coldly. "We're going to town, eagle feathers and all."

Bill Nunn had been a knife fighter all his life, preferring

the swift thrust or the thrown blade to any other way of combat. As he shuffled slowly toward the car, DeMarco's back was turned for the flick of an eye. The heavy knife left Nunn's hand, making a slow turn in the air, and buried itself to the handle under the agent's shoulder.

The blow drove DeMarco to his knees. He let out a sharp grunt of surprise and pain, strangled, and fell face down. His writhing ceased in less than a minute. Nunn dragged the body into the back of the dead man's car, avoiding the blood, and left it there with the eagle feathers.

The road that led to the abandoned limestone quarry a dozen miles from Pine Stump was as unused and lonely as the track at the end of which Nunn and DeMarco had kept their appointment. Nunn turned into it with headlights out, feeling his way along with the help of a waning moon that had come up at midnight.

There was an open space free of brush at the rim of the old quarry. He stopped there, a dozen feet from the drop, where bare rock sloped gently to the edge. The car would leave no telltale tracks to hint at what had happened.

Nunn stepped out, released the brake, and gave the car a hard push. It rolled over the rim, and he heard the splash as it hit the black water of the half-flooded pit. He turned away without a backward look, and began the walk back to the Pine Stump dump and his pickup. He was home and in bed before daylight.

He told Vachon nothing of what had happened, judging it safer to keep his own counsel. Vachon would have told him to clear out. He was a more sophisticated and educated man than the mountain-reared poacher, and he would have read the danger in the situation. Nunn did not. He was gambling that his tracks were covered and that the car at the bottom of the quarry would keep its dark secret as long as he lived.

It was Einar Malone, a broad-shouldered young conservation officer, who led State Police to the abandoned pit.

"Toll has been done in," he told them, "and Bill Nunn did it. The agent was after Nunn for shooting eagles and Bill is not the kind to hold still. He's the meanest character around here."

Malone knew enough about the country and the habits of the poacher to suspect exactly what had happened. He took police divers to the quarry and they located the sunken car on the third dive. Brought up, it yielded Toll's body and a gunny sack of eagle feathers.

The two officers who arrested Bill Nunn took no chances. They went to the house after dark, and when his slattern of a wife came to the door, gross and shapeless in a dirty cotton dress, they asked for him.

From the ill-lighted kitchen behind the woman, Nunn growled, "What the hell do you want?"

One officer stood framed in yellow lamplight from the door but the other was hidden in darkness a few steps away.

"Come out, Nunn," the nearer trooper ordered, "and if you've got a gun or a knife with you don't reach for it. We've got you covered front and back."

Nunn shuffled slowly to the door, but when the order came to put out his wrists for the manacles he balked.

"You ain't gonna take me in," he blazed. "I done a year down south when I was a boy, and I ain't goin' back to no goddam pen."

The officer hidden in the darkness spoke quietly. "You're either going in with us or you're going to the morgue. Take your choice. I'm holding a .38 on you, and we have Ike Toll's body. After what you did to him, I'd just as soon squeeze off as look at you. Ike was a cop and a damn good one. In our business we don't like cop killers."

Nunn was put away for good before the end of the summer, in the high-walled and grim prison at Marquette.

For all his surliness, there was in the makeup of this remorseless outlaw one inconsistent strain of sentiment. He loved the woods and cherished, without even putting the thought into words in his own mind, the wildness and freedom he found in them. Confinement he could not endure.

He was quartered in a cell tier three floors up, with a catwalk in front. Returning from the prison mess hall on a morning three months after he was sent up, he dived headlong from that catwalk to the concrete floor below.

He made no attempt to break his fall. He struck head foremost, with a noise like that of a ripe melon bursting. The guards who rushed to him found him beyond the need of any attention.

The eagle feather trade in the Lake Superior country died with him. Baldy Vachon was scared off, and there was no one else willing to take the risks for the paltry sums of money involved.

But the reprieve came too late to save the shrinking nesting population that was left.

THE CLOSING YEARS

When the female eagle died at Nunn's hands, leaving her half-incubated eggs in the nest, the cycle of hatching and rearing that had gone unbroken there for more than half a century was broken at last. There was no chance that Khan would remate that season.

In age, he was now the equivalent of a man in his seventies. The urge to mate was waning in him, but he missed the she eagle out of sheer loneliness, with an emotion much like that of a bereaved human.

He stayed in the vicinity for a month, solitary and moping, at times perching in his lookout tree or on the nest itself, ranging and hunting widely over the Sleeping Bear country. But in the end he drifted away, following the Lake Superior shore to the west.

Fifty miles from the Great Nest, among a cluster of timbered and unpeopled islands off a point jutting into the big lake, he found a place to his liking, and there he spent the remainder of the summer. Fish and water birds were abundant and the hunting was easy. Save for a vague discontent, begotten of the fact that there were no others of his own kind anywhere in the area, the weeks passed pleasantly for him.

Shortly after he arrived he discovered, in a swamp beside a small boggy lake on one of the larger islands, a nesting colony of great blue herons.

There were fifty nests, bulky and flat, flimsily built of twigs and small sticks, bedded at the end of slender branches in the very top of a dozen of the tallest trees. Some of the platforms were so thin and unsubstantial that when they had held eggs, earlier in the spring, a man looking up from the ground below could have seen the outline of the eggs through the poorly woven floor of the nest.

By the time Khan found the rookery, in late May, it teemed with activity and noise.

Save in their nesting season, the tall gray herons were birds of solitary habits. When they hunted fish and frogs and other prey, in the shallow water of small lakes or along the swampy shores of some secluded bay, or when they flew to and from their fishing grounds with slow and measured wingbeats, they were rarely seen in the company of another heron. Nor was there anything in their way of life to suggest that they would nest anywhere save on the ground in some isolated marshland retreat, each pair by itself, guarding jealously its isolation.

But when the time came for courtship and mating, the herons forsook their solitary ways completely. They gathered in crowded colonies and sought the tallest trees they could find for their nesting sites. The old birds returned year after year to the same swamp and even to the same nest, repairing and strengthening it. And the younger ones followed their parents back to the colony and built nests of their own, so that if no disaster overtook it the teeming treetop city grew larger year by year.

It was not unusual to find half a thousand nests in a single colony, and more than one towering swamp elm held in its top branches as many as thirty of the frail platforms, the highest often a hundred feet or more above the ground.

The herons seemed poorly designed for this treetop life. Their long, slender legs, accounting for almost half of their height, which lacked hardly more than a foot of reaching to a man's shoulders, served them ill when it came to perching. For all that, they never alighted on the nest itself, but rather on a slender branch nearby, a branch that swayed wildly with the force of their landing. They steadied themselves then with outspread wings until they achieved balance, when they walked gravely and deliberately to the nest, folded their stiltlike legs and settled on it.

A few weeks before Khan first saw the place, each of the platforms had held from three to six pale blue green eggs, faithfully attended by the two parent birds. They took turns at brooding, changing with regularity four times a day, shortly after daybreak, in midmorning and midafternoon, and again just before dark. Each of these changes brought a brief but beautiful display between the mated pair. Neck feathers and crown plumes lifted, long hackles on back and breast and throat erect and spread, the two confronted each other as if throwing down a challenge to angry combat. But after a few seconds the display subsided, the newcomer moved into place on the eggs with slow, careful steps, and the mate lifted and winged away in quest of food. That quest might take the bird as far as twenty miles from the rookery, but the herons had no betters at stalking and killing the prey they needed and there was little chance they would come back with empty craws.

The young birds were hatched now and the feeding visits of the adults went on hour after hour, by night as well as by day. They gulped down their prey where it was caught, flew back to the nest and regurgitated it for the fledglings. Long of leg and awkward, nevertheless the latter quickly learned to stand and grasp the bill of the parent in their own to receive the food.

Because of their diet of water creatures, the excrement of the young herons was the consistency and color of liquid white- wash. In eliminating it, they tried, as the young eagles did, to eject it beyond the rim of the nest. But they were conspicuously unsuccessful, so that the platform and the branches around it, as well as the ground below, were whitened long before the young birds were grown. And because the heron way of feeding re- sulted in much spilled food as well, for a man walking into the rookery by early June the stench was overpowering.

The heron colony was of no interest to Khan as a hunting ground. Taking either the young in the nests or the old birds in the tops of the trees would have been totally foreign to him, and although he flew above the swamp often he paid the herons not the slightest attention.

But the day came when he chanced on one of them at his fishing, standing tall and stately in shallow water on a marshy point, a graceful, lovely figure against the green of the bog and the summer blue of the pond.

In his own way, the heron was as skilled at his hunting as the eagle. He stood now with his neck curved back on his shoulders in a graceful letter S, long yellow bill poised like a javelin ready to be thrown, incredibly keen eyes scanning the shoals and shoreline ahead.

Even as Khan, cruising a mile away, slanted toward him, the heron saw prey of his own. It was a big watersnake, thick of body, muddy black in color, basking at the dry end of a half- submerged log along the shore.

The heron moved with incredible stealth, bending his long legs at the heel joint, moving one foot ahead of the other so carefully that the surface of the water did not show a ripple, gliding toward the snake as softly and silently as a shadow.

When he was within striking range, the blow of the javelin bill was a blur of motion too fast for the eye to track. The bill opened as it struck and the two mandibles gripped the snake firmly by the neck. The heron lifted the thrashing body, took a few quick steps to the shore, dropped his prey and stabbed it savagely in the head to kill it. The first blow stunned the snake but it still twisted and writhed, and before the bird could strike again he heard the tearing sound of cleft air and whirled to see the eagle stooping at him in a sloping dive.

There was no time for escape.

The heron crouched, feathers lifted and fluffed so that he looked twice his real size, his head drawn back like the head of a coiled diamondback. A harsh guttural squawk broke from his throat.

He was a picture of blind rage, and the threat was genuine. That heavy bill could kill the eagle if it found its target in an eye. At the last instant Khan aborted his attack. This was a bird bigger than he had ever struck, and more dangerous. He would kill it if he could, but not recklessly.

He braked his fall with fully opened wings and touched down just beyond the heron's reach. The tall wader made no effort to retreat. Instead, it faced its attacker like a swordsman ready to thrust, plumage bristling, crying hoarsely in mixed anger and fright.

The eagle lifted, hopping his own length into the air, feinting at his quarry with outspread feet thrust down for the clutch. But the long slender neck of the wader straightened and the bill drove to meet him with the sure swiftness of a rapier. Khan swerved aside.

He feinted half a dozen times, but the heron would not give ground and in the end the eagle broke off the attack. He rose above the marsh, climbing in wide spirals, and when he was no longer a threat the heron lowered his ruffled plumage and also took wing. His flight was measured, as it always was, but faster than normal, and he kept close to the ground in case the eagle returned. Khan had had enough of this tall swordsman, however. He had been bested for the first time in all his years by another bird, and not again in his lifetime would he look upon a great blue heron as prey.

Dave Barrows never learned what happened to the female

that had been Khan's mate for sixteen years. But when she disappeared, leaving eggs in the nest, and Khan also vanished from the Sleeping Bears, it was heartbreaking to him.

He had had the Great Nest under observation for more than twenty seasons now, and in that time he had come to know things about the eagles and their way of life that no man had ever before ferreted out. In addition, they had become almost a part of him, objects of an affection and understanding that was a very substantial element in his life.

He saw the interrupted nesting as signaling the end of the cycle of events he had watched so long, concluding that in all likelihood both birds of the old pair were dead, and he felt their loss much as one feels the loss of close friends. But in March a year later, his disappointment came to an end. Khan had found another mate.

She was a young female, one of a group of five birds, all that were left in Khan's wintering country. Immature and still in the brown plumage of her youth, she was nevertheless ready for courtship and nesting, and Khan did what the male eagle that had sired him had done many years before, when he himself was in his third spring. He wooed her and was accepted, and in March the two of them began together the leisurely flight north, to the Sleeping Bears and the nest in the tall pine.

Khan was an old eagle now, in his twenty-second year, and the fierce mating urge of his earlier springs was dying out. He courted his young mate with the old grace and ardor, but the consummation of their courtship was less urgent, and where he had once coupled many times in a single day, he was content now with brief and infrequent encounters on the platform of the nest. Nevertheless, the matings were sufficient to bring about the fertility of the two eggs the female laid in April.

Her own life-span was not yet sufficiently long for the poison residues in her food chain to build to critical levels in her body. That would come soon enough, but for this year she laid viable eggs, and in early May, when the pale green and silver veils of spring lay over the mountains, she hatched two eaglets.

The younger of the pair was frail and lived only a fortnight. The other, a lusty male, survived, trained for flight, and left the nest toward the end of summer. But before the winter ended he was dead, shot by an irresponsible hunter from a duck blind in a marsh almost a thousand miles to the south of the aerie where he had been fledged.

He was the last eaglet that would be produced anywhere around the Great Lakes. The doomed race was coming to its end. Barrows had record now of only one other active nest, and that one had sent no fledglings into flight for three seasons.

It was ironic, but not surprising when the fierce ways of these proud raptors were taken into account, that of the pitiable remnant of eagles left it should fall to Khan to destroy one and drive another into mateless banishment.

The intruders invaded his country on a warm morning in May, when his own young were only a few days old. They were a mated pair of young birds, but not nesting, and they were on an erratic and aimless flight from their home territory far to the north.

Khan watched them approach, sailing in wide spirals high above the greening mountains. When they came near enough he flew to give battle, voicing his challenge in wild screaming.

The two interlopers attacked together and for the first minutes of the battle the odds were long against him. But then his young mate, watching from the nest, left her fledglings and flew to join him, and the four eagles fought their savage aerial combat on equal terms.

It began high in the blue vault of spring sky, but they lost altitude as they tumbled and clashed, feinting at each other, stooping, barrel-rolling, turning back-down to present their mailed feet to the enemy. In the end they were barely above the treetops and the tide of battle had not turned in favor of either pair.

But now, so close to his own aerie, Khan drove home his attack with savage determination. He won a place above the younger male twice in swift succession and stooped as he would have stooped on a duck. The first time the other eagle tilted in the air and met him with outthrust feet. But the second stoop went home, dealing a numbing blow that left the victim half stunned. On the heels of it Khan clutched and the two birds eddied to the ground together.

They fought there like gamecocks, leaping at one another, buffeting and fending with their wings, striking with beaks and talons. In the end the young eagle would have fled had there been an opportunity, but Khan gave him no chance.

The old eagle broke through his opponent's guard at last and gained a place astride him, almost in the position of a mating pair. He reached then with his terrible feet and sank the curved claws deep in back and wing muscle, slashing and tearing. A wing of the younger bird drooped and failed, leaving him helpless, and Khan killed him as he would have killed prey, ripping at the thrashing body until it was still, hardly more than a clod of blood-stained feathers and slack flesh.

Overhead, the two females broke off their combat. Khan stood over the dead eagle for a moment, screaming his triumph. Then he lifted and he and his mate went back to the nest together, paying no further attention to the surviving stranger, retreating now over the distant ridges. But when she came back to their area the following day, searching for her lost mate, Khan rushed to attack once more, diving and screaming, and she fled in total defeat.

Thereafter the Sleeping Bear country would belong, for as long as they lived, to the eagles at the Great Nest.

THE STORM

At the end of his twenty-fourth summer the aging Khan and the young female that was his mate, now in her white plumage, went south, only to find no other bird of their kind anywhere in their winter country.

Along the big river where he had wintered with fifty other eagles less than twenty years before, there was not one left. The lone pair were by themselves at last, and before the time came for the return flight north in spring the she eagle died.

There was nothing splendid or dramatic in her death. Her eyes did not glaze in lethal combat, nor was she even struck down by the gun of an outlaw hunter.

Slowly she sickened from the poisons that had accumulated in her body in the six short years of her life, poisons she had taken in bite by bite with the flesh of the fish and waterfowl on which she lived. The last two springs she had laid thin-shelled eggs that broke under her feet before she could brood them. Now the deadly compounds had become too much for the brain and sturdy heart that kept her alive.

She sat listlessly for many days in a lookout tree, not leaving it even on short flights. She did no hunting. A few times Khan brought her food but she refused it. She grew gaunt and unkempt. In the end she left the perch and dropped down to the upturned stump of a fallen tree on the riverbank, sitting there without heed to the wide reaches of sky above her, where she had ruled as a queen all the brief span of her life. Her wings drooped, her head was hunched between her shoulders in an attitude of complete wretchedness, and the once fierce eyes turned more and more dull under the beetling brows. She died during a night of winter rain, slipping from the stump with no struggle. At daybreak she was a sodden lump of lifeless plumage on the river shore.

There was no female to replace her. Khan came back to the Great Nest alone in March. Around him on every side, to north and south, east and west, stretched more than six thousand miles of timbered shoreline along the vast inland seas that are the Great Lakes. Much of that country was wind-heaped dunes, cliffs, or rocky beaches, unpeopled and wild. Long reaches were miles distant from the nearest road or human habitation, unmolested by man. All this was eagle habitat and the great birds had once nested in most of it.

But now, in all that wild array of shore and water there was none left. Nowhere in it could Khan have found another of his own kind.

The poison sprays of the orchards and farms, the feather hunting, the heedless behavior of men who killed eagles for no better reason than that they were big and splendid and preyed on living things weaker than themselves—for all these reasons, the long succession of Khan's kind was ended in the Lake Superior country.

There were a few pairs of eagles still returning to aeries

inland, on the big flowages of Wisconsin, the interior lakes and rivers of Michigan and Minnesota, and along the bayous and backwaters of the upper Mississippi, their future uncertain and precarious. And far to the northwest, in Alaska and along the mountainous coasts of British Columbia, thousands still nested, feeding on the spent salmon that lay in putrid windrows on the sandbars of countless spawning streams.

Even on the treeless Aleutians far out to the westward, where tangles of dwarf birch no higher than a man's knees were the nearest approach to timber, eagles still built their aeries on jutting headlands that looked out to the sea, lining them with dry kelp and the dead stalks of wild celery.

But of the Great Lakes population that had once numbered in the hundreds, only the pied eagle survived, and none of the distant birds interested him. He was held by bonds too strong to sever to the nest where he had hatched, where he had mated through all his adult years, and where he had watched his own princelings grow to flight summer after summer. He had no wish to join another clan.

The great raptor had known the Sleeping Bear country as its sky lord for a quarter century. Now Khan was desolate. He stayed in the vicinity of the Great Nest for two months, a lonely and dispirited figure waiting to keep a rendezvous that could never come to pass, perched disconsolate for hours in his lookout tree or circling in the limitless solitude of the spring sky.

Did his heart break then, in the silent isolation of his survivorship? Did the fierce will to live that had flooded his body with every pulsebeat for a quarter of a century gutter and die out at last?

On a warm May morning not unlike the one that had witnessed his birth, he left the Sleeping Bears forever, flying north, out over the empty gray plain of Lake Superior toward some far-off place he had never seen.

From the blind at the top of the observation tower, Barrows watched him go with a strange presentiment that he would not see Khan again.

He had watched the solitary eagle intermittently since he returned from the south, fully aware that he was the last of the line. Earlier that same morning, through binoculars, Dave had made out clearly the worn aluminum band that he had fitted to the leg of the fledgling twenty-five years before.

In those years he had come to know a great deal about eagle ways, and about the hunting and mating and rearing of this unique pied bird that he had named Khan. But he realized as well that there was much neither he nor any other man would ever know, events that took place day after day beyond the reach of human eyes.

And that morning, seeing Khan diminish to a speck far out over the big lake, he felt he was losing a friend of long standing.

The eagle flew steadily, toward a big timbered island that lay in the lake fifty miles away. At first he saw it only as a blue smudge on the horizon. Then the terraced green ridges rose higher, and presently he was above them, cruising in wide circles, seeking prey. He was not long in finding it.

For more than an hour that morning, on an open slope of rock near the top of one of the ridges, a she lynx had lain at the entrance to her den, watching her three kits play in the sun. The den was under the arched roots of an ancient stub killed by lightning many years before, and the mother lay in their shadow, where her soft gray fur matched her surroundings so faultlessly that not even the marvelous eyes of an eagle could make her out.

The kits had been born in early March. They were the size of small housecats now, with thick fur shorter than their mother's, as full of play and mischief as domestic kittens. Although they still suckled at the she lynx's dugs, they were beginning to relish as well the warm red flesh of the snowshoe hares and squirrels and grouse she carried to them. In a few more weeks they would be ready to learn the business of hunting for themselves.

Two of them wearied of romping and retired into the dark sanctuary of the den. The third continued to frisk, rolling on the sun-warmed ground like a ball, chasing its tiny stub of a tail, seeking to entice its mother out to join in the frolic. But she had killed a rabbit at daybreak, the second of the night, and was too full to be interested in sharing the play of her young.

Khan, flying a few hundred feet above the timber, saw the small lynx. He came about in a tight circle, tilted and banked, and stooped in a vertical dive with the windless air shrieking past his folded wings.

The kit squalled like a young domestic cat as the eagle's talons sank into its soft body, and the she lynx sprang from beneath the roots of the stub in a gray blur.

For the wild things as for man, fear of death is the ultimate fear. But in the flesh eaters, including the birds of prey, once combat is joined with an enemy a battle rage wells up that blots out that fear and blinds them to all but the lust to kill. So it was now with Khan.

In all the battles he had fought in the twenty-five years of his life, he had confronted no adversary so terrible as this snarling, raging mother lynx. But he felt no fear of her and he was not aware of pain.

He tilted backward and thrust his feet out to meet her, but she dodged aside and evaded them, and before the eagle could regain his balance she had sunk her teeth deep under one wing and her claws were raking his breast and back, tearing away skin and plumage, ripping long cuts in his flesh.

There was swift death in those flailing claws and the eagle knew it. He tried to lift and his wings carried him off the ground to the height of a man's head. But the lynx kept her hold and her weight bore him down again.

The duel could not be of long duration, for it was not in the nature of either feline or bird to play a role of caution or delay the final outcome. One or the other must die. It would be decided quickly and the loser would not quail.

It was over in minutes. Khan drove the curved talons of one foot into the flank of the lynx, found her vitals and tore open a wound that would kill her. But by that time she had done terrible damage to the breast muscles that powered his wings, so that he was half disabled. He was not able to rise into the air again, and as he weakened she slashed at his head, clawing out an eye. Then, moving with the swiftness of a striking snake, she closed her jaws at the back of his neck, dealing the death blow her kind liked best.

A stain of blood obscured the patch of white plumage in his breast now. The great wings that had breasted the air currents above mountain and forest and farmland in a dozen states beat a slow last tattoo against the ground, and the fierce, implacable eyes that had scanned a thousand lakes and rivers for prey began to glaze. The proud head sank and came to rest on sun-warmed rock in front of the lynx den, and the final tremor of death ran through the strong body.

The saga of the strangely marked eagle, begun so many years before in the tall pine by Siskowet Lake, was ended.

Khan died on a day when the timbered country of the north had reached the apex of its vernal loveliness, with trees decked in the soft green of young foliage and wildflowers covering the forest floor with a bright tapestry.

The night that followed was one of extraordinary beauty, and vibrant with wilderness sound. The moon rose at dark, round and full, its radiance slanting down in shafts through the treetops so that black shadows alternated with patches of moonlight on the ground. Every lake and pond and stream course in the mountains was veiled with ethereal ribbons of silver mist.

At dusk whippoorwills had begun their pulsing calling, and from beaver ponds and bogs treefrogs sounded a ringing chorus of sweet and birdlike trills. In the half-darkness a white-throated sparrow sang his plaintive threnody over and over, and as the moon floated up a pair of loons called in wild ecstasy from the upper end of Siskowet Lake.

Had a man been camped beside a dying fire anywhere in

the mountains that night, he would have found the beauty of the place almost too much to endure. But for a dozen miles in every direction no man saw that beauty or listened to the night sounds. That was part of the spell the Sleeping Bears cast.

The change came shortly after midnight. It began with flashes of distant lightning and the rolling mutter of thunder far off in the southwest. Black clouds climbed the sky, edged with silver where the moon struck them, as beautiful as they were ominous. Then the storm swept in over the mountains, drenching the earth with rain and bending the trees in a gale of wind, and the moon was gone.

The bolt of lightning that struck the aerie pine forked across the black sky in a blinding flash of light. It fingered the topmost branches, high above the eagle nest, and there was a rending, splitting sound, drowned out in an earthshaking crash of thunder, as the hollow trunk parted in a long wound that ran from crown to roots.

The wind leaned the riven tree far out from the face of the cliff, and at last the weight of the huge nest, weight it had borne for over half a century, was too great. The pine snapped on its stump like a broken matchstick and fell, slowly at first, then in a plunging cartwheel. It crashed on the rocks at the bottom of the overlook, and at daybreak nothing remained of the Great Nest but a rain-sodden pile of rubble, scattered among the green branches of the fallen top. The aerie that had served him all his life had outlived Khan by less than a day.

In the heap of sticks and earth at the base of the cliff, a small white object caught the morning sun. It was a strange thing to have a place in the broken nest of an eagle, the stained and crumbling skull of a mink.

It had lain there all the years since it had fallen from the flesh of the bird that had sired Khan, in the summer after he was born, unseen by human eyes but speaking mutely of the wild fierce ways of all the eagles of the earth, of the pitiless laws that rule their realm of sky and solitude.